Unveiled

The Grave Whisperer

Angeline Gallant

Published by Crest & Quill Press, 2024.

UNVEILED

First edition. November 19, 2024.

ISBN: 979-8230241348

Written by Angeline Gallant.

Table of Contents

MARY ATKINSON

MARY ATKINSON[1]

When Mary passed away in 1827, Kingston, Ontario, was a thriving settlement and a key military and trading hub in Upper Canada. Life during this period was defined by a blend of colonial expansion, political evolution, and economic development. Here's a snapshot of what life was like at the time of Mary Atkinson's death:

Social and Cultural Life

Population: Kingston was growing steadily, with a mix of British Loyalists, Indigenous peoples, and immigrants from Scotland, Ireland, and England. It served as a melting pot of cultures, influencing social customs and traditions.

Housing: Most homes were modest wooden or stone structures, often reflecting Georgian architectural influences. Families relied on open fireplaces for cooking and heating.

Community: Churches like St. Paul's Anglican Church were vital centers of spiritual and community life, providing social cohesion in the settlement.

ECONOMY

Kingston's economy revolved around the fur trade, agriculture, and shipping. Its location on Lake Ontario made it a strategic point for transporting goods.

Small industries, like milling and blacksmithing, supported the local population. Markets in Kingston provided essential supplies, with trade continuing to expand.

POLITICAL CLIMATE

Upper Canada was experiencing significant political development. The Family Compact, a conservative oligarchy, controlled much of the colony's administration. However, this dominance was beginning to face resistance from reformist groups.

The tensions between reformists and loyalists were quietly brewing, which would later influence Canadian political history.

DAILY LIFE AND CHALLENGES

Health: Medical knowledge was limited, and diseases like cholera and tuberculosis were prevalent. The lack of sanitation in many areas contributed to health challenges.

Women's Role: Women like Mary Atkinson were central to family and community life. They managed households, supported their families, and played active roles in church and charity work.

Education: Education was becoming more accessible, with small schools opening in settlements, though it remained a luxury for many families.

HISTORICAL CONTEXT

1827 marked the early stages of a shift toward modernization in Upper Canada. Canals, like the Rideau Canal (begun in 1826), were under construction to improve transportation and military strategy.

Kingston, with its prominent military presence, was part of broader efforts to fortify the colony and secure trade routes.

MARY ATKINSON'S LIFE and death occurred during a transformative time in Kingston's history, as it evolved from a frontier settlement into a cornerstone of Upper Canadian society. Her burial beneath St. Paul's Church speaks to the enduring legacy of those who shaped the early years of the city.

WILLIAM ATKINSON

WILLIAM ATKINSON[2]

William Atkinson passed away in Kingston in 1825, at a time when the city was cementing its role as a vital military and economic hub in Upper Canada. His final resting place beneath what is now St. Paul's Anglican Church places him among the early settlers and contributors to Kingston's rich history.

Life in Kingston in 1825

Community Growth: Kingston's population was steadily increasing, with more settlers arriving from Europe and the United States. As a Loyalist stronghold, it maintained strong ties to British culture and governance.

Economy: Trade on the Great Lakes was flourishing, with Kingston serving as a key port. The town's economy was supported by agriculture, milling, and small industries, alongside its military garrison.

Military Presence: Kingston's importance as a military center continued to shape its identity. The British military maintained a significant presence, contributing to the town's infrastructure and economy.

DAILY LIFE AND EVENTS

Religion and Community: Churches like St. Paul's were cornerstones of daily life, offering spiritual guidance and acting as hubs for social gatherings and charitable work.

Health Challenges: As in most of Upper Canada, outbreaks of diseases like smallpox and cholera remained a constant threat. Limited medical knowledge meant that life expectancy was relatively low.

Transportation: Roads were still rudimentary, and waterways like Lake Ontario and the St. Lawrence River were the primary means of travel and trade.

HISTORICAL CONTEXT

Political Climate: The colony was experiencing shifts toward self-governance, with debates about land distribution and political representation gaining traction.

Infrastructure Development: The construction of the Rideau Canal had begun in 1826, with Kingston playing a significant role in this ambitious project designed to secure trade routes and military access.

WILLIAM ATKINSON'S life and death reflected the realities of this era—a time of resilience, growth, and transformation for both Kingston and the broader colony. His burial, now part of the foundations of St. Paul's Anglican Church, ensures his legacy remains intertwined with the city's historical fabric.

WILLIAM ATKINSON ESQ.

WILLIAM ATKINSON, ESQ.[3]

William Atkinson, Esq., was a prominent figure of his time, married to Mary Badgley. His life and contributions were deeply rooted in Kingston, Upper Canada, where he was interred on April 10, 1805. His grave, now part of the foundation of St. Paul's Anglican Church, places him among the earliest pioneers who shaped the city's burgeoning identity.

Life in Kingston in 1805

Emerging Urban Center: Kingston was a small but vital settlement in Upper Canada. Its strategic location along Lake Ontario made it a focal point for trade, military operations, and Loyalist migration.

Loyalist Influence: The town remained a hub for United Empire Loyalists, who had fled the American Revolution to rebuild their lives in British territory. Their values and traditions continued to shape the city's governance and culture.

Economic Activity: Agriculture, small industries, and trade were the mainstays of Kingston's economy. The town's position as a port facilitated connections with other settlements and trading posts along the Great Lakes.

RELIGIOUS AND SOCIAL Life

Faith and Community: Churches like St. Paul's played a critical role in the spiritual and social life of early Kingston residents. Religious observance was central to daily routines, and community gatherings often revolved around the church.

Colonial Challenges: Life in 1805 was not without hardship. Disease, limited medical care, and the physical demands of pioneering life tested the resilience of settlers.

HISTORICAL CONTEXT

Colonial Expansion: Upper Canada was in the early stages of its development as a British colony. Land grants were being distributed, and settlements like Kingston were integral to the colony's growth.

Military Significance: The British military's presence ensured Kingston's defense and contributed to its infrastructure, including roads, forts, and public buildings.

WILLIAM ATKINSON'S interment in Kingston's St. Paul's Anglican Churchyard marked the passing of an individual whose life was intertwined with the early history of the city. His legacy endures, preserved beneath one of Kingston's most historic landmarks.

WILLIAM ATKINSON

WILLIAM ATKINSON[4]

William Atkinson, a resident of Kingston in the early 19th century, passed away in 1813. His parentage remains a mystery, adding a layer of intrigue to his story and the lives of those who settled in this fledgling community. His final resting place now lies beneath St. Paul's Anglican Church, a structure built over the graves of many early pioneers.

Life in Kingston in 1813

War of 1812 Impact: Kingston was a strategic military post during the ongoing War of 1812. The town served as a supply and naval base, with Fort Henry under construction to bolster defenses against American forces. Tensions were high, and the war shaped daily life for residents.

Economic Pressures: The conflict disrupted trade routes and strained resources. Essential goods were scarce, and many families faced economic hardship.

Community Growth: Despite the challenges, Kingston continued to grow, with settlers establishing homes, businesses, and farms, contributing to the town's resilience.

LEGACY BENEATH ST. Paul's

William Atkinson's interment in the churchyard in 1813 places him among the many whose lives helped build Kingston into a vital Upper Canadian settlement. His grave, now part of St. Paul's Anglican Church, reflects the lasting bond between the community and its past.

As the city expanded, these early pioneers became part of its foundation—literally and figuratively—through their enduring contributions and the stories they left behind.

Atkinson's unknown origins highlight the enigmatic nature of genealogy, prompting questions about the journeys and lives of those who helped shape Kingston's history.

ROBERT WALTER ATKISON aka ATKINSON

ROBERT WALTER ATKISON aka ATKINSON[5]

Robert Walter Atkison, also known as Atkinson, passed away in Kingston in 1812. Like many early settlers, his parentage remains unknown, adding another mystery to the history of Kingston's early years. He was laid to rest in the churchyard of what would later become St. Paul's Anglican Church, a place that now holds the stories of numerous pioneers who helped shape the community.

Life in Kingston in 1812

War on the Horizon: The War of 1812 erupted, bringing uncertainty and fear to Kingston. The town became a crucial British military hub due to its strategic location along Lake Ontario and proximity to American borders.

Naval Developments: As tensions rose, shipbuilding efforts in Kingston surged, with the Royal Navy establishing a fleet to defend against American forces.

Community under Stress: Residents endured rationing and disruptions in trade as the war effort demanded resources. Yet, the community banded together, showcasing resilience during difficult times.

LEGACY BENEATH ST. Paul's

Robert Walter Atkison's grave, now beneath St. Paul's Anglican Church, symbolizes the sacrifices and contributions of those who lived during turbulent times. His life and death serve as a reminder of the fragility and strength of the settlers who laid Kingston's foundations.

With the passage of time, the church and its grounds have become a repository of history, guarding the secrets and legacies of individuals like Atkison, whose stories are intertwined with the fabric of early Canadian life.

JOHN AUSTIN

JOHN AUSTIN[6]

John Austin passed away in Kingston in 1816, his life marking another chapter in the story of early Upper Canada. He was interred in the churchyard that would later be the site of St. Paul's Anglican Church, a sacred ground preserving the memory of Kingston's pioneers and settlers.

Life in Kingston in 1816

Post-War Reconstruction: The War of 1812 had ended just a year earlier, leaving the town in a phase of rebuilding and reflection. Kingston, having been a key military and naval center during the war, now focused on restoring trade and community life.

Economic Recovery: With peace restored, Kingston experienced slow but steady economic growth, as shipping and commerce began to recover on Lake Ontario. Farmers and merchants sought to rebuild their livelihoods after years of conflict.

Civic Developments: Efforts to organize and formalize civic structures increased. Churches, schools, and small businesses began to flourish as the town's population grew and adapted to peacetime needs.

LEGACY BENEATH ST. Paul's

John Austin's grave, now beneath St. Paul's Anglican Church, represents the quiet contributions of individuals who lived through both war and peace. Though details of his life remain unknown, his final resting place connects him to the story of a community persevering in the wake of hardship.

St. Paul's Anglican Church continues to stand as a testament to the lives and legacies of those like Austin, preserving the memory of Kingston's past for future generations.

REBEKAH AUSTIN

REBEKAH AUSTIN[7]

Rebekah Austin passed away in Kingston in 1816, joining the many early settlers interred in the grounds that later became part of St. Paul's Anglican Church. With no surviving record of her parents, her life story remains a poignant mystery, representative of the many unnamed and little-documented individuals who helped shape early Upper Canada.

Life in Kingston in 1816

Community Growth: Despite the challenges following the War of 1812, Kingston was steadily evolving from a military stronghold into a bustling town. New settlers arrived, contributing to the social and cultural fabric of the community.

Role of Women: Women like Rebekah often played critical yet undocumented roles in their families and communities. They managed households, supported agriculture, and engaged in small-scale trade, all essential for survival in a frontier town.

Healthcare Struggles: Life expectancy was often cut short by diseases such as tuberculosis, cholera, and other ailments for which medical understanding was limited. The year 1816, known as "the year without a summer," brought crop failures and food shortages, further stressing communities.

A LEGACY IN ST. PAUL'S Churchyard

Rebekah Austin's final resting place beneath St. Paul's Anglican Church is a testament to the many unsung lives that laid the foundation for Kingston's future. Her story, though incomplete, echoes in the annals of history, reminding us of the resilience and sacrifice of early settlers.

W. AYKROUD aka AYKROYD

W. AYKROUD aka AYKROYD[8]

W. Aykroud, also recorded as Aykroyd, tragically passed away as an infant in Kingston in 1812. With no documentation of his parents, his brief life leaves behind little more than a name, underscoring the fragility of life in the early 19th century. His grave, now beneath St. Paul's Anglican Church, serves as a quiet reminder of the countless children lost to the hardships of that era.

Life in Kingston in 1812

War of 1812: Kingston was a strategic military hub during the war, with heightened activity around the naval dockyard and Fort Henry. The community was marked by both the tensions of conflict and the resilience of its inhabitants.

Child Mortality: The early 19th century saw high infant mortality rates due to diseases like smallpox, dysentery, and respiratory infections. Limited medical knowledge and poor sanitation contributed to these tragedies.

A Frontier Community: Families in Kingston during this time often faced the dual challenges of survival and growth, relying on close-knit communities and shared resources to endure the difficulties of frontier life.

A NAME PRESERVED

Though his life was fleeting, W. Aykroud's burial site beneath St. Paul's Anglican Church reflects the collective history of Kingston's earliest days. His name, like those of many others, has been preserved, offering a glimpse into the personal stories that shaped the town's development.

SARAH BADGLEY

SARAH BADGLEY[9]

Sarah Badgley was laid to rest in Kingston on May 6, 1804. Like many others of her time, details about her family and lineage have been lost to history, leaving only her name and burial record to mark her existence. Her grave lies beneath St. Paul's Anglican Church, where her memory continues to resonate as part of Kingston's rich historical tapestry.

Life in Kingston in 1804

A Growing Settlement: By 1804, Kingston was an important settlement in Upper Canada, benefiting from its strategic location on the St. Lawrence River and its proximity to Lake Ontario. The population was expanding, with Loyalist families establishing roots and contributing to the town's development.

Community and Faith: Churches, including the future site of St. Paul's, played a central role in daily life, serving not only as places of worship but also as community centers. Burial sites were often closely associated with these sacred spaces.

Challenges of the Era: Life remained difficult, with families facing the persistent threat of illness, limited medical care, and the demanding labor required to build homes, farms, and infrastructure in the growing town.

A LEGACY BENEATH THE Stones

Sarah Badgley's story, like that of many buried at St. Paul's Anglican Church, reflects the quiet contributions of individuals who helped shape Kingston's identity. Though little is known about her life, her presence endures beneath the church's foundation, a reminder of the many lives interwoven into the fabric of early Upper Canada.

WILLIAM BADGLEY

WILLIAM BADGLEY[10]

William Badgley was buried in Kingston on March 20, 1798, at a time when the town was still in its formative years, developing rapidly as the new century began. His grave lies beneath the grounds of St. Paul's Anglican Church, a site that has become an enduring part of Kingston's history. Unfortunately, like many individuals of the period, details surrounding his life and family have been largely lost to time, but his final resting place remains a testament to his presence in the early days of this growing community.

Life in Kingston in 1798

A Town on the Rise: Kingston was emerging as a key location in Upper Canada, thanks in part to its role as a military garrison. The town was strategically important, sitting on the St. Lawrence River and overseeing trade routes. It was a time of significant change, as the British military, Loyalists, and new settlers worked to establish the foundation for the future of the province.

Building a New Community: As the town expanded, so did its institutions, with churches becoming central places of worship, community gathering, and, for many, their final resting places.

Challenges of Survival: For many residents of Kingston in 1798, life was defined by the struggle to survive in a harsh environment. Smallpox outbreaks, limited medical knowledge, and the tough realities of pioneering life meant that many families faced loss and hardship.

A SILENT MARKER OF History

Though little is known about William Badgley's life, his burial site beneath St. Paul's Anglican Church speaks volumes about the role of early settlers in shaping Kingston. His name is one of many etched into the history of the region, a silent marker of a time when the town was still in its infancy. His grave, along with countless others, forms the foundation of the church, which itself is a cornerstone of the community's history.

WILLIAM BAIN

WILLIAM BAIN[11]

William Bain passed away in Kingston in 1823, his final resting place now beneath the hallowed grounds of St. Paul's Anglican Church. At the time of his death, Kingston was continuing its evolution from a military outpost to a thriving community, still bearing the marks of its colonial past while pushing toward a new, more settled future.

Life in Kingston in 1823

A Town in Transition: By 1823, Kingston had grown into a vital center of commerce and governance in Upper Canada. It was the seat of the Legislative Assembly for the province, and its strategic position along the St. Lawrence River made it an essential hub for trade and communication. However, Kingston was still developing its identity, balancing its British military roots with the influx of settlers from various backgrounds.

A Struggling Post-War Economy: The War of 1812 had only ended a decade prior, and its impacts were still being felt. Many families faced economic hardships and were working to rebuild from the financial strains caused by the conflict.

Faith and Community: St. Paul's Anglican Church, constructed around this time, became a symbol of both spiritual and community life in Kingston. It was a place of comfort and solace for the residents, providing not only religious services but also a gathering place for social connection during a time when many were still adjusting to life in a developing colonial town.

A LIFE MARKED BY TIME

Although the specifics of William Bain's life remain elusive, his place in Kingston's history is cemented beneath the church that continues to serve the community today. The grave is a quiet reminder of the individuals who lived, struggled, and contributed to the growth of this region in its early years. His legacy, like so many others, is interwoven with the town's foundations, his story part of the rich tapestry that has shaped Kingston into the city it is today.

CHARLES BAKER JR.

CHARLES BAKER JR.[12]

Charles Baker Jr. passed away in Kingston in 1823, and his final resting place lies beneath the hallowed grounds of St. Paul's Anglican Church. His death during this period places him within a pivotal time in Kingston's history, a moment of transition from military outpost to emerging urban center in Upper Canada.

Life in Kingston in 1823

Kingston's Growth and Development: In 1823, Kingston was a town in the midst of transformation. It had grown steadily since its establishment as a military post and had become the capital of Upper Canada before the capital was moved to Toronto in 1841. During this time, Kingston remained a key location for trade and military defence, with its strategic position on the St. Lawrence River. The completion of infrastructure projects and the rise of local commerce and industry began to shape its future as a regional center.

A Young Community: Despite being a town with a rich colonial past, Kingston in 1823 was still adjusting to the increasing presence of settlers. The population was diverse, with both Loyalists and newer arrivals from Britain and other parts of the world. This diverse influx of people and their blending cultures would define much of the town's social fabric in the years to come.

St. Paul's Anglican Church: By this time, St. Paul's Anglican Church was an important landmark for Kingston's residents. Built to serve a growing Anglican community, it became a symbol of stability in an ever-changing town. It offered spiritual solace and a place of gathering in the early days of Kingston's growth, especially important for families like Charles Baker Jr. 's, who were embedded in the town's formative years.

CHARLES BAKER JR.'S Legacy

While details of Charles Baker Jr.'s life remain limited, his burial in St. Paul's Anglican Churchyard signifies his connection to the town and its community. His passing in 1823 reflects the lives of many early settlers who helped lay the foundation for the vibrant Kingston that would emerge in the coming decades. His presence, interred in the churchyard, is a reminder of the many lives that contributed to the town's character, even as their stories slowly faded with time.

As part of the historical narrative of Kingston, Charles Baker Jr. represents the unknown lives that shaped the town—ordinary yet essential figures whose footprints continue to echo in the very places they once lived and died.

HANNAH MARIA BAKER

HANNAH MARIA BAKER[13]

Hannah Maria Baker passed away in Kingston in 1815, and her final resting place lies beneath the hallowed grounds of St. Paul's Anglican Church. Her life, though shrouded in the mists of time, reflects the experiences of women in early 19th-century Upper Canada—an era marked by emerging communities, the formation of local identities, and a growing sense of independence within the confines of colonial society.

Life in Kingston in 1815

Post-War Transition: In 1815, Kingston was adjusting to life after the War of 1812, a conflict that had deeply impacted the town, given its strategic location on the Great Lakes. The end of the war brought some stability to the region, but Kingston still felt the lingering effects of the military buildup and the wartime economy. The town began to recover and rebuild, slowly transitioning from a military town into a civilian settlement.

Economic Growth and Infrastructure: Kingston's position as an important trade and military hub continued to bolster its economic significance. By 1815, the town was seeing the early stages of urbanization, with local markets, farms, and businesses helping to solidify the town's role in Upper Canada's development. Infrastructure projects, like roads and public buildings, started to reshape Kingston's layout, with St. Paul's Anglican Church standing as a central institution in this transformation.

Religious and Social Life: Religion played a central role in the lives of the people of Kingston during this time. The Anglican community, in particular, was deeply rooted, and St. Paul's Anglican Church served not just as a place of worship but also as a social and communal gathering spot. For women like Hannah Maria Baker, the church was a place of comfort, support, and connection—a way to maintain stability in a rapidly changing world.

HANNAH MARIA BAKER'S Legacy

Though the details of Hannah Maria Baker's life remain largely unknown, her burial in St. Paul's Anglican Churchyard speaks to the enduring presence of women in the shaping of early Kingston. It was a community where religious institutions provided solace, and where women like her played key roles in maintaining the social fabric of early Canadian settlements. Women's roles during this period were often overlooked in historical records, yet their contributions to family, community, and local life were immeasurable.

Hannah's death in 1815, just a few years after the War of 1812, marks her as part of a generation that lived through tumultuous times, yet continued to form the backbone of a growing town. Her burial site beneath St. Paul's Anglican Church serves as a reminder of the countless, often unnamed, individuals whose lives and deaths were part of Kingston's early history. Each life, though not always remembered in detail, contributed to the larger story of Upper Canada and the enduring legacy of the town.

CPT. JAMES BAKER U.E.L.

CPT. JAMES BAKER U.E.L.[14]

Captain James Baker, a United Empire Loyalist, passed away and was laid to rest in Kingston on April 11, 1800. His grave now lies beneath St. Paul's Anglican Church, a landmark that stands as a silent witness to the lives of many Loyalists who sought refuge and new beginnings in Upper Canada after the American Revolution.

As a Loyalist, Captain Baker's life reflected the turmoil and resilience of those who remained loyal to the British Crown during a time of great upheaval. Following the revolution, he and others like him contributed to the establishment of a thriving Loyalist community in Kingston, a strategic military and naval hub. His burial in what became St. Paul's Anglican Church underscores his prominence and the critical role Loyalists played in shaping the early history of Upper Canada.

St. Paul's, constructed decades later, stands as a testament to Kingston's evolution and the lives of those who built its foundations. Beneath its floors lie stories of courage, loyalty, and transformation, woven into the fabric of Canada's early identity. Captain James Baker's final resting place ensures his legacy endures, connecting the past with the present.

MATTHEW BALFOUR

MATTHEW BALFOUR[15]

Matthew Balfour, born on August 18, 1818, to John Magauley Balfour and Mary Ann Day, had a tragically brief life. He passed away just over a month later, on September 30, 1818, and was laid to rest in Kingston. His grave, like many others, now lies beneath St. Paul's Anglican Church, a historic site that holds the stories of Kingston's early settlers.

Matthew's passing highlights the fragility of life in the early 19th century when infant mortality was heartbreakingly common. Families faced harsh realities due to limited medical knowledge and resources. Despite their sorrow, the Balfour family's story is a reminder of the resilience of Kingston's early residents who built lives and legacies during this challenging era.

St. Paul's Anglican Church, built decades later, stands as a solemn guardian of these early graves, preserving the memory of infants like Matthew and the families who mourned them. It is a place where history and humanity intersect, offering a glimpse into the lives and struggles of those who came before.

JULIA BALLAN aka BALLOND

JULIA BALLAN[16]

Julia Ballan, also recorded as Julia Ballond, was laid to rest in Kingston, Upper Canada, on November 11, 1796. Her burial site, like many others from Kingston's early days, now lies beneath the historic St. Paul's Anglican Church.

The late 18th century was a transformative period in Kingston, as settlers and Loyalists worked to establish a thriving community despite numerous challenges. Life at the time was marked by frontier hardships, limited access to medical care, and the ever-present influence of political change following the American Revolution.

Julia's burial predates the construction of St. Paul's Anglican Church, which later became a significant landmark. Her grave, alongside those of other early settlers, contributes to the tapestry of Kingston's history. The church now serves as both a place of worship and a memorial to those who played a role in shaping the region's foundation, preserving their stories for future generations.

CHARLES BAMFORD

CHARLES BAMFORD[17]

Charles Bamford passed away in 1826 in Kingston, Upper Canada. His final resting place now lies beneath St. Paul's Anglican Church, a historical landmark built over the graves of many early settlers.

By the time of Charles Bamford's death, Kingston was a bustling hub of commerce and governance in Upper Canada, benefiting from its strategic location by Lake Ontario. The construction of infrastructure such as roads and public buildings was helping the community grow, and the local economy thrived on industries like shipbuilding, trade, and agriculture.

St. Paul's Anglican Church, constructed shortly after this period, became a spiritual and cultural center. Beneath its foundation lie the remains of individuals like Charles Bamford, whose lives and contributions are etched into the history of Kingston and Upper Canada. His grave and others provide a poignant connection to the city's early settlers and their enduring legacy.

JOHN BARNES

JOHN BARNES[18]

John Barnes was laid to rest in St. Paul's Anglican Churchyard on October 21, 1803. His grave, along with many others, was later encompassed by the foundation of St. Paul's Anglican Church, constructed to serve the growing community in Kingston, Upper Canada.

At the time of John Barnes' burial, Kingston was evolving as a central settlement in Upper Canada. As a prominent Loyalist hub, the town was characterized by its mix of military presence, trade activities, and the development of civic institutions. The churchyard where Barnes was interred was a significant burial site for the town's early residents, reflecting the community's need for a spiritual and communal space.

The eventual construction of St. Paul's Anglican Church over these graves symbolized the community's growth and its reverence for those who had shaped its early years. John Barnes' internment in this historic site connects him to the fabric of Kingston's foundational history.

JANE BARNS

JANE BARNS[19]

Jane Barns was laid to rest in Kingston, Upper Canada, on April 23, 1803. Her burial took place in what was then a growing settlement, marked by its strategic importance as a Loyalist stronghold and a developing community hub. Over time, the churchyard where Jane was buried became the site of St. Paul's Anglican Church, a reflection of the community's expanding spiritual and social needs.

Life in Kingston at the time of Jane's passing was defined by its Loyalist roots, as settlers worked to rebuild lives after the American Revolution. The town was a mix of military operations, burgeoning commerce, and the establishment of essential institutions like schools and churches. The construction of St. Paul's Anglican Church over the burial ground in later years honored early settlers like Jane, preserving their legacy as part of Kingston's history.

JOSIAH BARRICE

JOSIAH BARRICE[20]

Josiah Barrice was interred on October 24, 1795, in Kingston, Upper Canada. His burial took place in a period of early development for the settlement, which was a significant Loyalist enclave following the American Revolution. As settlers established roots in the area, cemeteries like the one where Josiah was buried served as reminders of the hardships and sacrifices faced by those building new lives in a frontier environment.

In subsequent years, St. Paul's Anglican Church was constructed over this burial ground, symbolizing the growing importance of religion and community in Kingston. The church became a focal point for the town, embodying the resilience and determination of pioneers like Josiah. His grave, now beneath the foundation of St. Paul's, connects his story to the broader narrative of Kingston's evolution from a Loyalist outpost to a key center in Upper Canada.

JOHN BATEMAN

JOHN BATEMAN[21]

John Bateman was laid to rest in Kingston, Upper Canada, on April 28, 1811. This was a time when Kingston was transitioning from a Loyalist stronghold into an important military and trade hub in Upper Canada. The town's population was growing, and with it, the need for spiritual and communal spaces like St. Paul's Anglican Church.

Built later over the burial ground where John Bateman rests, St. Paul's Anglican Church symbolizes the convergence of faith, history, and the stories of early settlers. Bateman's burial site reflects the lives of those who helped lay the foundation for Kingston's development, their sacrifices now part of the church's enduring legacy. His resting place beneath St. Paul's reminds us of the close ties between the people and the landmarks that shaped the community.

UNKNOWN BAYMANS aka BAYMAN

UNKNOWN BAYMANS[22]

The unknown Baymans, also recorded as Bayman, was a child laid to rest on May 13, 1810, in Kingston, Upper Canada. This was a period when childhood mortality was tragically common due to diseases, lack of advanced medical care, and harsh living conditions in the developing colony. The child's identity may be lost to time, but their burial reflects the struggles and resilience of families striving to build lives in the early settlement.

The construction of St. Paul's Anglican Church over this burial site transformed the area into a sacred space, intertwining the histories of those buried there with the spiritual and communal life of Kingston. The unknown Baymans now rest beneath the church, a poignant reminder of the countless untold stories that shaped Upper Canada's past.

JAMES BAYMAN

JAMES BAYMAN[23]

James Bayman was laid to rest in Kingston, Upper Canada, on November 17, 1799. His life and death occurred during a transformative period in the region's history, when Kingston was developing as a central hub of trade, governance, and military activity in Upper Canada. The challenges of frontier life often brought hardships, and the burial of individuals like James Bayman reflects the reality of a community that balanced growth with personal loss.

St. Paul's Anglican Church, later constructed over the churchyard where James Bayman was buried, serves as a lasting tribute to those early settlers. Their graves now lie beneath the foundation of a building that became a cornerstone of Kingston's spiritual and cultural heritage. James Bayman's memory, though largely lost to history, remains an integral part of this legacy.

ADAM BEARD

ADAM BEARD[24]

Adam Beard was buried in Kingston, Upper Canada, on October 15, 1805. During this time, Kingston was a growing town at the heart of the British colonial presence in Canada, a place where military fortifications, trade routes, and settler communities intersected. Adam Beard's passing reflects the challenges and early life in this developing region, where the struggle for survival was often intertwined with the expansion of British rule.

St. Paul's Anglican Church, which was later built over his grave, stands as a testament to the enduring faith and resilience of the early settlers of Kingston. As time passed, the church grew to become not just a place of worship but also a central landmark that connected generations to the past. Adam Beard's resting place beneath its foundation is a quiet, enduring part of Kingston's early history—one of many individuals who helped shape the community, even as their names faded from the records of time.

CPT. ANTOINE MARTIN BEAUBIEN

CPT. ANTOINE MARTIN BEAUBIEN[25]

In 1756, Captain Antoine Martin Beaubien was born in Quebec, New France, during a period of immense change and conflict in North America. Quebec, at the time, was a French colony in the midst of the Seven Years' War (1756–1763), a global conflict that pitted the French and their allies against the British and their own colonial forces.

Life in New France was shaped by the challenges of colonial existence: the harshness of the environment, the need for strong community bonds, and the pressures of survival and defense. Quebec was a relatively small but strategic area with a mix of French settlers, Indigenous peoples, and French military presence. The French colony was primarily agrarian, with a focus on fur trading, farming, and the Catholic faith, which played a central role in daily life.

As the conflict of the Seven Years' War began to escalate, tensions between the British and French colonists grew. The British had been gradually expanding their territorial ambitions in North America, and New France became a significant flashpoint. The year 1756 marked the beginning of the French and Indian War, a North American theater of the larger Seven Years' War, where French forces fought alongside various Indigenous groups against British colonial forces.

For young Antoine Martin Beaubien, this would have meant growing up in a society that was under constant threat of conflict and surrounded by war. Quebec was not only a hub of French culture and Catholicism but also a militarized outpost, with the French seeking to defend their lands from British encroachment. The Beaubien family, likely part of the French settler elite, would have been involved in the social and economic activities of the time, whether in trade, military service, or land management.

By the time Beaubien came of age, the outcome of the war had already been decided, with the Treaty of Paris (1763) ceding New France to the British. This seismic shift would have profoundly impacted his life and the future trajectory of the Beaubien family, as they navigated the complex and often dangerous waters of British rule in Quebec.

WHEN CAPTAIN ANTOINE Martin Beaubien was three years old in 1759, the Industrial Revolution had not yet reached its full force, but it was on the horizon. The Industrial Revolution is typically dated to begin around the late 18th century, roughly in the 1760s to 1780s, in Britain, and it gradually spread to other parts of the world, including the Americas, during the 19th century.

At the time of Beaubien's early childhood in Quebec, the world was still predominantly agrarian, with the vast majority of people living in rural areas and working in agriculture or small-scale crafts. In New France, society was centered around fur trading, farming, and Catholicism. The area's economy was driven by agriculture, with settlers cultivating crops and raising livestock, alongside the booming fur trade which was crucial to the colony's survival and growth.

However, across the Atlantic in Britain, the Industrial Revolution was beginning to reshape the global landscape. While it had yet to impact Quebec directly, this era marked the beginning of profound changes in technology, society, and economy that would eventually reverberate across the world. These changes included:

1. Technological Innovations: The invention of the steam engine by James Watt in the 1770s, as well as new manufacturing techniques,

began the shift from hand production to machine-based manufacturing, especially in textiles, iron, and coal mining. These developments transformed the way goods were produced, leading to the rise of factories and the decline of traditional cottage industries.

---

2. URBANIZATION: IN Britain, the rise of factories and mass production led to the growth of cities and a shift from rural to urban living. People began migrating to urban areas in search of work in factories, drastically altering societal structures.

---

3. TRANSPORTATION: Innovations like steam-powered engines in railroads and ships started to make long-distance travel faster and more efficient. This revolutionized trade, allowed goods to move more easily, and helped spread industrialization to other parts of the world.

WHILE ALL OF THIS WAS unfolding in Britain, in Quebec, the effects were less immediate. New France was still deeply engaged in the effects of the French and Indian War, and by the time Beaubien was in his early adulthood, New France had become a British colony (post-1763). The industrial changes of the early 19th century began to have some effect on Quebec's economy, but the region was more isolated from the industrial centers of Europe and the American colonies for some time.

It wasn't until much later in the 19th century that the Industrial Revolution started to reach full force in Canada. Cities like Montreal and Toronto began to industrialize, with factories, railroads, and urbanization transforming the landscape, but that would happen long after Captain Beaubien's youth.

Thus, while he may not have experienced the Industrial Revolution firsthand, Beaubien's life spanned the early years of a changing world, and by the time he passed away, Canada was beginning to embrace the changes that would shape the modern industrial world.

CAPTAIN ANTOINE MARTIN Beaubien's service in the Royal Canadian Volunteers places him in a significant historical context during a pivotal time in Canadian history. The Royal Canadian Volunteers was a militia unit formed in the late 18th century, particularly during and after the American Revolution. It was part of the efforts by the British to maintain control over Canada and defend the territory from American forces.

Born in 1756, Beaubien would have witnessed the tumultuous period of the American Revolution (1775-1783) in which many French Canadians, like himself, were caught between loyalty to the British Crown and the growing calls for American independence. The Royal Canadian Volunteers was made up of French-Canadian settlers, like Beaubien, who were enlisted to defend British interests in Canada. Their role was vital during this period, especially as many Loyalists (those loyal to the British Crown) fled the Thirteen Colonies and resettled in Canada, where tensions with the American revolutionaries remained high.

Beaubien, having joined the Royal Canadian Volunteers, likely participated in military actions along the frontier, particularly in the defense of Quebec and the St. Lawrence River Valley. His service would have helped secure British control of what would later become Canada, at a time when conflicts like the American Revolution and the War of 1812 were shaping the future of North America.

His rank as a captain suggests that he was trusted with leadership responsibilities, overseeing troops and likely engaging in key military operations, particularly during the post-Revolutionary War period when tensions with the United States remained. After the conclusion of the Revolution, Beaubien's military expertise would have been valuable during the era of settlement and the establishment of new communities in Canada.

By the time Beaubien reached adulthood, Canada was undergoing significant transformation, with French and British colonial interests still competing in the region. His military career as a captain in the Royal Canadian Volunteers placed him in the midst of a developing Canadian identity, one that would continue to evolve over the coming decades as the region sought to define its place on the world stage.

Beaubien's service in the militia, and his life in the early years of Canada's history, would make him a part of the complex tapestry of military, social, and political change that marked the transition from New France to British North America. His experiences would have shaped his perspectives as the fledgling country began to establish itself amid the growing conflict with the United States.

IN 1783, WHEN CAPTAIN Antoine Martin Beaubien was 26 years old, the world witnessed a monumental event in the history of aviation: the first successful flight of a hot air balloon. This flight, carried out by the Montgolfier brothers, Joseph-Michel and Jacques-Étienne, in France, marked a groundbreaking achievement in the quest for human flight.

The Montgolfier brothers had been experimenting with the concept of lighter-than-air flight, using hot air to inflate a large fabric balloon. On June 4, 1783, they successfully launched the first manned flight in a balloon made of cloth and paper, powered by hot air, from Annonay, France. The flight lasted for about 10 minutes, reaching an altitude of 1,000 feet (300 meters). Later, in September 1783, the first successful human flight was achieved when Jean-François Pilâtre de Rozier and François Laurent d'Arlandes ascended into the sky in a balloon over Paris.

This event was one of the key milestones that sparked the fascination with air travel, paving the way for future innovations in aviation. However, in the 18th century, such technological feats were still relatively rare, and the implications of human flight were not immediately understood. The world was still in the midst of the Enlightenment, an era that valued scientific discovery and intellectual progress.

While Beaubien himself was likely not directly involved in the ballooning phenomenon, he would have heard of these advancements. At the time, Quebec (and much of the world) was still a land influenced by more traditional, terrestrial ways of life, especially in colonies like New France and Upper Canada. Beaubien's early adulthood coincided with the dawn of these remarkable technological and scientific breakthroughs that would eventually reshape the world.

Though air travel would not become practical or widely accessible until well into the 20th century, the successful flight of the Montgolfier brothers would have sparked imaginations across the globe, including that of young Beaubien, who lived through a period of rapid scientific and industrial change.

CAPTAIN ANTOINE MARTIN Beaubien's burial in Kingston on April 13, 1800, places him at the end of a significant chapter in early Canadian history. His death occurred in the aftermath of the tumultuous years of the American Revolution, a time when the region of Upper Canada (now Ontario) was still in its formative stages as a British colony.

In 1800, life in Kingston, which was a small but strategically important military outpost at the time, was still defined by British military presence and the ongoing settlement of Loyalists who had fled the United States following the Revolution. The town was slowly emerging as a center of governance and commerce within the province, especially as tensions with the United States continued to simmer, leading up to the War of 1812.

The late 18th century saw the British fortifications in the area, particularly Fort Frontenac (near present-day Kingston), being critical for controlling the Great Lakes and the fur trade. As a captain in the Royal Canadian Volunteers, Beaubien would have played a role in maintaining British authority over the region and contributing to the defense of the colony.

By the time of his death in 1800, the shift from military conflict to peaceful settlement was taking shape in Kingston, though challenges remained. The town was a vital location for governance, trade, and military activity. For Beaubien, whose life was intertwined with both military duty and the early Canadian colonial experience, his death in Kingston marked the end of one era and the beginning of another.

St. Paul's Anglican Church, which would later be built over his grave, became a symbol of the changing cultural and religious landscape in the area. The Anglican Church was one of the dominant religious institutions in Upper Canada, and its construction in Kingston marked a shift toward more permanent settlements and the establishment of British institutions in the region. Beaubien's burial under St. Paul's serves as a reminder of the region's military past, the settlement of

Loyalists, and the British legacy that would define much of early Canadian history.

As with many early settlers, Beaubien's life and death are embedded in the story of how Upper Canada transitioned from a military frontier into a thriving, albeit still vulnerable, colony. His service in the Royal Canadian Volunteers, his role as a captain, and his burial in Kingston all highlight the importance of this period in the development of what would become Canada.

WILLIAM BEEMAN

WILLIAM BEEMAN[26]

William Beeman's burial on June 5, 1799, in Kingston, Upper Canada, places him in the midst of a transformative time in Canadian history. At the close of the 18th century, Kingston was a small but significant British military post, a hub of strategic importance due to its location along the St. Lawrence River and its proximity to the American border. Life in Kingston at that time was defined by the aftermath of the American Revolution, during which many Loyalists—those who remained faithful to the British crown—settled in the area to establish new lives in the wake of their displacement.

The late 1700s in Kingston were marked by British military fortifications, such as Fort Frontenac, and the growing presence of Loyalist families who contributed to the development of the town and surrounding areas. Kingston itself was gradually transitioning from a primarily military garrison to a more permanent civilian settlement, with its religious and social institutions taking shape.

Beeman's burial during this period reflects the struggles and hopes of the Loyalist settlers who helped lay the foundations for Upper Canada. As with many others, Beeman would have faced the challenges of establishing a new community in a recently formed colony that was still feeling the effects of war, but also beginning to prosper due to the stability provided by British rule. The year 1799 was still a period of transition for Kingston, with the town starting to develop into a key settlement in Upper Canada.

The construction of St. Paul's Anglican Church, which would eventually be built over Beeman's grave, was a major milestone in the spiritual and community life of the area. The Anglican Church was the established religion of the British settlers, and its presence in Kingston marked the increasing institutionalization of British governance and culture in the region. By the time the church was built, the settlement was evolving into a more established community, and its church would serve as a center of both religious and civic life for the people of Kingston.

Beeman's life and death are quietly interwoven into the early history of Kingston, Upper Canada, and the broader story of Loyalist migration and settlement in the wake of the American Revolution. His burial in Kingston, under the future site of St. Paul's Anglican Church, symbolizes the founding generations that helped shape the region's transition into the British colonial framework that would evolve into the nation of Canada.

JOHN BELFLEUR

JOHN BELFEUR[27]

John Belfleur's burial on February 26, 1805, in Kingston, Upper Canada, places him during a pivotal time in the region's history. As a Loyalist settlement, Kingston was growing and transforming from a military stronghold into a more permanent community in the early 19th century.

The first years of the 19th century were marked by the aftermath of the American Revolution. Many of the Loyalists who had fled to Upper Canada in the late 18th century were working to build a new life in the midst of the challenges posed by a relatively young colonial society. Kingston was an important location for the British due to its military fortifications, notably Fort Frontenac, and its strategic position along the St. Lawrence River, making it a focal point for settlement, trade, and defense.

By 1805, the town had begun to establish the foundational structures that would support its growing civilian population. The building of St. Paul's Anglican Church, which would eventually stand over Belfleur's grave, symbolized both the religious and cultural ties to the British crown, as the Anglican faith was dominant among the Loyalists. The church would become not only a place of worship but a social and civic center for the community.

John Belfleur's death in 1805 represents the lives of many early settlers who had helped establish the growing town and were integral to its development. The fact that St. Paul's Anglican Church was built over his grave ties him to the foundational period of Kingston's growth and marks his place in history as part of the Loyalist legacy in Upper Canada.

During this time, Kingston was still in the process of building infrastructure, with many homes and businesses still in the early stages of development. The area around St. Paul's Church, which became a key institution for both religious and community events, was an integral part of the evolving social fabric of the town. Life in Kingston during the early 19th century would have been centered around the church, the fort, and the waterfront, with many settlers working to create stability and community in their new homeland.

Belfleur's burial in such a significant location, under the future St. Paul's Anglican Church, highlights his connection to the community's foundational years and serves as a reminder of the generations of settlers who contributed to the shaping of Upper Canada's early history. His life and death reflect the challenges and resilience of the Loyalists who made Kingston their home and laid the groundwork for the future of the region.

ROBERT BETSON

ROBERT BETSON[28]

Robert Betson's burial on October 28, 1805, in Kingston, Upper Canada, places him in a time of transformation for both the town and the broader region. The early 19th century marked a period of significant change, with Kingston transitioning from a military outpost to a thriving civilian settlement. As a Loyalist stronghold, Kingston had been a place of refuge for those who had remained loyal to the British crown during the American Revolution, and many of these settlers were involved in shaping the community's growth.

By 1805, Kingston's economy was largely centered around trade, with the St. Lawrence River being a major route for transportation. The construction of St. Paul's Anglican Church, which would later be built over Betson's grave, symbolized both the town's British heritage and the growing role of religion in the life of the community. Anglicanism, as the established church of the Loyalists, played a central role in daily life, with the church becoming a key social institution as well as a place of worship.

Robert Betson's burial during this period speaks to the lives of many early settlers who were working to create stability and community in Upper Canada. Life in Kingston during the early 1800s was marked by the construction of buildings, roads, and other infrastructure, as well as the continuing establishment of a strong British colonial presence. The town was also an important military location, with Fort Frontenac overseeing the region and providing security for the settlers.

St. Paul's Anglican Church, which was being constructed during this time, would later serve as both a place of worship and a cultural hub for the people of Kingston. Betson's connection to the church, through his burial site, ties him to the foundational years of the town. His grave represents not only his own life but also the lives of many other settlers who were establishing their new homes and laying the foundation for the future of the town.

The churchyard, which later became the site of St. Paul's, was an important focal point for the community, marking the town's growth and its commitment to building a stable, enduring society. Robert Betson's place in this early chapter of Kingston's history highlights the resilience and determination of the settlers, and his grave, located beneath the church, is a silent testament to the lives that helped build the town into what it would eventually become.

COMO DAVID BETTON

COMO DAVID BETTON[29]

Como David Betton, born in England, passed away in Kingston, Upper Canada, on October 11, 1794. His life spanned a time of significant change, both in the world and within the young colony of Upper Canada. By the time of his death, Kingston was already developing from a strategic military outpost into a more settled civilian community.

As a Loyalist who had likely been involved in the American Revolution, Como David Betton's death reflects the lives of many who had been displaced during the turmoil of the war. The Loyalists who settled in Kingston in the late 18th century had experienced great upheaval, as they fled the newly formed United States to remain loyal to the British Crown. Kingston, with its fortifications and strategic location on the St. Lawrence River, became a central location for the Loyalists in Upper Canada.

During this period, life in Kingston was still largely shaped by military presence and the establishment of British colonial authority. Fortifications such as Fort Frontenac were key to ensuring the safety of the town, and the construction of essential infrastructure, such as roads and bridges, was beginning to transform the area into a more cohesive community.

St. Paul's Anglican Church, which would later be built over Betton's grave, was central to the social and religious life of the early settlers. For many of the Loyalist settlers, Anglicanism was more than just a religion—it was a symbol of their allegiance to the British Crown and an important part of their cultural identity in the new land. As Kingston's first Anglican church, St. Paul's would become the spiritual heart of the town, its construction signaling a commitment to the British traditions of the Loyalist community.

Betton's burial site under what would become St. Paul's Church connects him directly to this formative period in Kingston's history. His resting place, marked by the church, tells the story of the early Loyalist settlers who helped build the foundations of Upper Canada. Their struggles, hopes, and contributions were central to the development of the community, and the church—now built over their graves—serves as a lasting monument to their legacy.

ANN BLACKWOOD

ANN BLACKWOOD[30]

Ann Blackwood was buried in Kingston, Upper Canada, on May 3, 1805, during a period of growth and transition for the region. Kingston, strategically located on the shores of Lake Ontario and the St. Lawrence River, was increasingly becoming a hub for both military and civilian life, particularly for the Loyalist population who had settled in the area after the American Revolution.

By 1805, the town was still a relatively small community, but it was beginning to take shape as a key military outpost and emerging colonial center. The establishment of St. Paul's Anglican Church, built over Ann Blackwood's grave, speaks to the central role religion played in the lives of the settlers. The Anglican church would have served as a place of spiritual solace and a focal point for the social and cultural identity of the British Loyalists in the area.

Life in Kingston at the time was centered on the growth of infrastructure, including roads, bridges, and buildings necessary for a burgeoning community. The presence of the British military remained strong, as Fort Frontenac was a key part of the defense strategy, ensuring safety in a time of heightened tensions between British and American interests.

As for Ann Blackwood herself, her burial in the churchyard ties her to the early days of Kingston's settlement and the Loyalist heritage that would influence the community for generations. The construction of St. Paul's Anglican Church on top of her grave not only marks her final resting place but also serves as a lasting reminder of the people who lived, died, and contributed to the development of Upper Canada during this formative time in its history.

GEORGE BLAIN

GEORGE BLAIN[31]

George Blain, a sailor, was buried in Kingston, Upper Canada, on May 22, 1810. At that time, Kingston was a pivotal military and naval center on the Great Lakes, making it a fitting resting place for someone of Blain's occupation. The town's strategic location at the confluence of Lake Ontario and the St. Lawrence River made it an essential site for naval activities, particularly as tensions between the United States and Britain were escalating, leading into the War of 1812.

As a sailor, George Blain would have been part of the Royal Navy or a merchant fleet operating on the Great Lakes, which were crucial to both military and trade routes. The Royal Navy was active in defending British interests in North America, and Kingston's naval dockyards and forts played a key role in supporting these operations. It's likely that Blain's work, either as a sailor on a warship or a merchant vessel, contributed to the development of the region's economy and defense.

The construction of St. Paul's Anglican Church over his grave serves as a testament to the town's growth and the important role of religion in the community. The church, built in the early 19th century, became a gathering place for the settlers, and its graveyard would have been a final resting place for many of the town's early inhabitants, from soldiers and sailors to civilians.

George Blain's burial reflects the challenges and determination of the time—he was one of the many individuals who helped shape the early days of Kingston. His grave, marked by St. Paul's Anglican Church, offers a quiet reminder of the town's maritime past and the lives of those who helped it grow into the center it would become during the War of 1812.

GEORGE BLOOM

GEORGE BLOOM[32]

George Bloom passed away in Kingston, Upper Canada, in 1813. During this period, Kingston was a significant hub for British military operations, especially as the War of 1812 raged between the United States and Great Britain. Kingston's strategic location on Lake Ontario, its proximity to the U.S. border, and its strong military presence made it a key site for British forces.

In 1813, Kingston served as a vital base for the Royal Navy and British Army, with its fortifications and naval dockyards crucial to the defense of Canada. It was a year marked by intense military activity, with significant battles taking place, such as the American assault on the town of York (now Toronto), and British counterattacks. While George Bloom's exact role is unclear, as a resident of Kingston during this time, he would have lived through these turbulent events.

Being buried in the graveyard of St. Paul's Anglican Church places George Bloom's resting place in the heart of Kingston's early history. As one of the town's early settlers, his grave under this prominent church suggests he was part of the community that built the foundations of the town in its early years. The church itself was not only a spiritual center but also an important marker of Kingston's growing urban landscape, with the churchyard serving as a final resting place for many of the town's pioneers and soldiers.

Bloom's burial in 1813, at the height of the War of 1812, reflects the intersection of civilian life and military tensions during that era. His presence in St. Paul's Anglican Churchyard reminds us of the people who contributed to the shaping of Kingston during a time of conflict and change, as the town moved from its colonial roots toward becoming a more established and fortified community.

UNKNOWN BOINTON

UNKNOWN BOINTON[33]

Unknown Bointon, a child buried in Kingston Upper Canada on August 10, 1804, represents one of the many young lives lost during this era. In the early 1800s, life in Upper Canada, especially in towns like Kingston, was marked by hardship, including the challenges of infant mortality and the impact of disease. The population of Kingston was still relatively small, and many families were part of the early settler communities trying to establish themselves in a rapidly changing and often unstable environment.

The period from the late 18th century to the early 19th century in Kingston was also a time of military activity due to its strategic location on Lake Ontario and the ongoing tensions surrounding the War of 1812. The town had become a key military stronghold for British forces, and the growing presence of settlers and soldiers alike created a complex environment for those living in the area.

As a child, Unknown Bointon would have experienced a different life than most adults—her passing likely reflecting the fragility of life during this time. The burial at St. Paul's Anglican Churchyard, with its historical connection to Kingston's military and civilian past, provides a solemn reminder of the town's early settlers and their families. With many of these early graves long forgotten, her resting place beneath St. Paul's Anglican Church signifies the many untold stories of the early inhabitants of Kingston.

Her grave, though nameless to us today, is a small but meaningful part of the broader tapestry of Kingston's history. It reflects the resilience of the community, the love of parents who mourned their child, and the changing face of the town as it grew into a major Canadian city.

EUGENIA BOINTON

EUGENIA BOINTON[34]

Eugenia Bointon, who was buried on August 31, 1804, in Kingston, Upper Canada, represents one of the many early lives interred in the town's first cemetery. The year 1804 was a time of transition in Upper Canada, with settlers attempting to make a new life in an area still reeling from the effects of conflict and the challenges of colonial existence.

Kingston itself, situated on the shores of Lake Ontario, was growing as both a military and administrative center, and St. Paul's Anglican Church, which would later be built over the graves of many early Kingston residents, served as a focal point for the community. It's likely that Eugenia's burial reflects the tough realities of life in the early 19th century, where many lives were cut short by disease, malnutrition, or accidents.

Her resting place beneath the future site of St. Paul's Anglican Church provides a connection to the town's history. The church became not only a spiritual center but also a historical landmark, witnessing the evolution of Kingston from a frontier settlement to an important city in Upper Canada. While the details of Eugenia's life remain unknown, her grave symbolizes the countless stories of the early settlers, each contributing to the legacy of Kingston's development and the story of a growing nation.

Her presence at St. Paul's, though largely forgotten over time, is an enduring part of the community's foundation, as every burial in the churchyard tells the tale of the individuals who shaped Kingston's history, even in ways that we may never fully understand.

CATHERINE ANNE BONNYCASTLE

CATHERINE ANNE BONNYCASTLE[35]

In 1829, Catherine Anne Bonnycastle was born into a period of significant transformation in Upper Canada, which would later become Ontario. The year marked the early stages of a time when the region was transitioning from a predominantly agrarian society to one that would embrace growing industrialization and urbanization in the coming decades.

The Political Landscape

Upper Canada was still a British colony at the time, with a governor appointed by the British Crown overseeing colonial matters. The colony was under the influence of British colonial policies, and tensions were rising as settlers grew increasingly dissatisfied with the political system, which favored British-appointed elites over the elected representatives of the people. In 1829, Upper Canada had not yet experienced the major political upheavals of the 1837 Rebellions, but the seeds of discontent were being planted. The colonial administration was entrenched, and many settlers, especially those from the Loyalist background, felt a growing desire for more local autonomy.

Economic and Social Life

The early 19th century in Upper Canada was a time of expansion, with settlers moving westward, establishing farms, and building communities. Kingston, where Catherine was born, was an important military and administrative center for Upper Canada. By 1829, Kingston had already grown from a fort town into a bustling port city, thanks to its strategic location along Lake Ontario and the St.

Lawrence River. The city had been a center for military activity, especially during the War of 1812, and it continued to play a key role in the trade routes that connected Upper Canada with Montreal and beyond.

The economy of the time relied heavily on agriculture, with farming families producing wheat, corn, and livestock to support the local population. However, Upper Canada was also beginning to see the early signs of industrialization, with mills, ironworks, and manufacturing starting to take root in places like Kingston. Despite this early industrial progress, most people were still dependent on agriculture for their livelihood.

Catherine's Family Background

As the daughter of Sir Richard Bonnycastle, a British army officer and a prominent figure in Upper Canada, and Frances Johnston, Catherine Anne Bonnycastle would have been born into a well-established, socially influential family. Sir Richard Bonnycastle was known for his military service and his contributions to colonial administration. He was an important figure in the construction of Fort Henry in Kingston and had a role in the development of various military infrastructure projects. Frances Johnston, his wife, was likely from a prominent Loyalist family, as many of the established families in Upper Canada had connections to the American Loyalist cause during and after the American Revolution.

Growing up in such an environment, Catherine Anne would have been exposed to the world of British military life, social events, and a strong sense of loyalty to the British Crown. Her family would have participated in the social fabric of Kingston, with access to the elite circles of society, including other military families, colonial officials, and businessmen.

Kingston in 1829

By 1829, Kingston had a population of around 5,000 to 6,000 people, and it was becoming one of the major urban centers of Upper Canada. The town was famous for its military importance, its port, and the nearby Fort Henry, which protected the area from potential attacks. The city had already experienced the building of important infrastructure, such as the construction of roads and canals, and there was growing trade with both the United States and Britain.

However, Kingston's social life, while expanding, would have been a world apart from the rural farming communities of Upper Canada. Life in Kingston was dominated by the military, government offices, and the elite, which is where Catherine Anne's family would have found their place. The Bonnycastle family likely lived in a comfortable, well-appointed home, and Catherine Anne would have been part of the British colonial elite, educated in manners, social expectations, and possibly even languages like French and Latin.

Summary of Life in 1829 for Catherine Anne Bonnycastle

Political climate: Upper Canada was under British control, and tensions over colonial governance were beginning to build, though the Rebellions of 1837 were still years away.

Economy: The economy was still agricultural, but the first signs of industrial growth were emerging. Kingston was an important port and military hub.

Family background: Catherine Anne's family was socially and politically connected, as her father, Sir Richard Bonnycastle, was a prominent military officer with influence in the colonial administration.

Kingston: Kingston was growing in importance as a regional center, and life there was relatively prosperous for families like Catherine Anne's, with access to elite social and political circles.

FOR CATHERINE ANNE, life in 1829 would have been shaped by the privileges of her family's status, surrounded by military, political, and social influence in a town that played a significant role in Upper Canada's development.

GEORGIANA BONNYCASTLE'S birth in 1832 and her untimely passing in 1833 would have been a heart-wrenching event for the Bonnycastle family, especially for Catherine Anne, who was only 2 years old at the time. As Catherine grew up, she would have likely been aware of her sister's brief life, perhaps through family stories or memories of the tragedy.

Life of Catherine Anne after Georgiana's Birth and Death

Catherine's Early Years: With Georgiana's birth, Catherine Anne would have experienced the early years of siblinghood, albeit briefly. At just 2 years old, Catherine would not have had full understanding or memory of the loss, but the absence of Georgiana could have been felt deeply by her parents, especially her mother, Frances Johnston Bonnycastle. The loss of a child was often devastating for families in that era, and it would have likely shaped the Bonnycastle family's emotional life.

The Bonnycastle Family's Grief: During this period, child mortality rates were high due to disease, malnutrition, and lack of modern medicine. The death of a child, especially so young, was not uncommon but always sorrowful. For a family like the Bonnycastles, who had social standing and a sense of duty to maintain their public image, the loss may have been deeply private, yet impactful on their household dynamics.

Catherine's Relationship with Georgiana: As Catherine was so young when Georgiana passed away, it is likely that any memory of her sister would have been faint. However, there could have been family memories of Georgiana that would later form part of Catherine's own legacy. As Catherine matured, stories of her late sister might have been shared, keeping Georgiana's memory alive in some form.

Family and Social Life: Despite the sorrow, Catherine's life would have continued under the watchful eye of her prominent father, Sir Richard Bonnycastle, and the structured, often military-dominated social life in Kingston. Catherine would have likely been sheltered from much of the grief, as families of the elite would often continue with their public duties, social engagements, and military activities, even in the wake of personal loss.

IN SUM, THE BRIEF LIFE of Georgiana Bonnycastle would have had a lasting emotional effect on Catherine, even if she did not have many direct memories of her sister. The Bonnycastle family would have carried the memory of Georgiana with them, and Catherine would have grown up in a world where the loss of a sibling was part of her family's history, subtly influencing her own development.

WITH THE BIRTH OF LOUISA Bonnycastle in 1833, just a few months after Georgiana's death, Catherine Anne would have been in the early stages of her childhood, still quite young at just 3 years old. The family, still grieving Georgiana's passing, would have likely experienced a complex mix of emotions at Louisa's birth, with joy for the new child tempered by the sorrow of losing their first daughter.

Life of Catherine Anne with the Birth of Louisa

Catherine's Early Childhood in a Time of Grief: At 3 years old, Catherine would have had a developing sense of her world but would have likely not fully understood the depth of the grief surrounding Georgiana's passing. However, she might have noticed the emotional atmosphere in the household, as parents often mourn for the lost child even as they welcome a new one. Louisa's arrival would have brought new energy to the family, and Catherine would have become more aware of her role as the older sister, even at such a young age.

The Bonnycastle Family in York, Ontario: At the time, York (now Toronto) was becoming an increasingly important administrative and social center. The Bonnycastle family, with Sir Richard Bonnycastle's military and civil responsibilities, would have been familiar with the bustling environment of the growing town. Catherine's life, as part of a prominent family, would have been shaped by the societal expectations of the time—gentlemanly conduct, social gatherings, and a focus on family heritage. The birth of Louisa could have also meant a new chance for the Bonny Castles to look to the future with renewed hope, even amidst the grief of the past.

Catherine's Relationship with Louisa: Catherine, at 3 years old, might have developed a sense of protectiveness toward Louisa as they both grew up. The arrival of a healthy sister after the loss of Georgiana could have brought comfort to the family, particularly to Frances Johnston Bonnycastle, who likely experienced the joy and sorrow of motherhood in equal measure. For Catherine, Louisa's presence may have filled the emotional void left by Georgiana's passing, offering her a bond with a new sibling in a world that was already familiar with loss.

Family Dynamics and Societal Expectations: Despite the personal sorrow, Catherine would have been expected to participate in the life of an upper-class family, attending to her social education, which would likely include receiving formal instruction in the arts, language, and etiquette. Louisa's birth would have added a new dynamic to the family, and Catherine might have been groomed to help care for her younger sister as they grew older. The Bonnycastle family would have moved forward with their life, balancing personal loss and the continuation of their social responsibilities in York.

IN ESSENCE, CATHERINE'S early life was marked by the shadow of grief from Georgiana's passing but also by the potential for a fresh start with the arrival of Louisa. As she matured, her role within the family would evolve, with Louisa likely becoming a close companion and the two sisters growing up together in a rapidly changing society. Their shared history would have connected them even more deeply as they navigated the complexities of life in 19th-century Upper Canada.

AT 7 YEARS OLD IN 1837, Catherine Anne Bonnycastle would have been at an age where she could begin to grasp the significance of the events unfolding around her, even if she may not have fully understood the political implications of the Upper and Lower Canadian Rebellions. However, as part of a prominent family, she would have been exposed to the tension and anxiety of those living through the turmoil.

Life for Catherine Anne Bonnycastle During the Rebellions

Political Upheaval in Upper Canada: The Rebellions of 1837 in Upper and Lower Canada were the result of growing dissatisfaction with British colonial rule, particularly regarding the lack of democratic rights, political representation, and economic inequality. While Catherine, at her young age, would not have been involved in the political turmoil, she would certainly have been aware of the unrest through her family's reactions. As the daughter of Sir Richard Bonnycastle, a prominent military officer and civil servant, she would have been living in an environment affected by these significant events.

Catherine's Family Role: As a daughter of a respected military family, Catherine's father, Sir Richard Bonnycastle, may have been called upon for his expertise during this time. As a man involved in the colonial military, he might have had responsibilities related to maintaining order or responding to the insurrection in some way. Catherine might have witnessed her father's involvement in military matters, and the gravity of the situation would have been apparent to her. Her mother, Frances Johnston Bonnycastle, would likely have taken measures to protect her children and ensure their safety during the unrest, keeping the household calm as much as possible.

Atmosphere in Kingston: Kingston, where the Bonnycastle family resided, was an important military and political hub during this time. Although Kingston did not see widespread fighting during the rebellions, tensions would have been high, and news of the violence and uprisings in places like Toronto and Montreal would have spread. For young Catherine, this could have been an unsettling period, as she would have witnessed the worry and fear of adults around her, along with the anticipation of what the outcome might be.

Catherine's Awareness of the Rebellions: Although Catherine was still very young, her exposure to the happenings of the time would have likely been significant. Her father's role in the military could have made her more aware of the threats posed by the rebellions, as families like hers were often directly impacted by political unrest. The Bonnycastles, being part of the loyalist establishment, would have had a vested interest in seeing the rebellion quelled. While Catherine might not have understood the full scope of the causes of the rebellion—like the grievances of the Patriotes in Lower Canada or the discontent in Upper Canada—she would have sensed the palpable anxiety and tension in her home and community.

Impact on Catherine's Childhood: The rebellion period would have disrupted the usual rhythm of life in Kingston and across Upper Canada. There may have been disruptions in schooling, or public events might have been cancelled as military and political priorities took precedence. As a young girl, Catherine might have experienced the suppression of her usual activities—perhaps less time with friends or play outside—and more focus on family matters, safety, and maintaining appearances. The fear of possible unrest, even if Kingston itself wasn't a major battleground, would have affected her everyday life.

Catherine's Relationship with Her Siblings: During the 1837 Rebellions, Catherine's bond with her sister Louisa would have been especially important, as their family navigated a period of instability. The two young girls would have likely found comfort in each other during this time. Catherine, still a child, would have relied on her family for security, and the maternal presence of Frances would have been a source of reassurance as Catherine tried to understand the tensions in her world.

Educational Impact: The rebellion may also have affected Catherine's schooling. She would have likely attended a private school or received education at home, and during this time of uncertainty, there may have been disruptions in her learning. The focus of education could have been adjusted to account for current events, with discussions about the political state of the colonies and the Rebellions potentially taking place in her home. It was a time when the political and military history of the land was unfolding, and she could have overheard adults speaking about it.

SOCIAL CHANGES IN UPPER Canada

For Catherine, the political upheaval of the Rebellions could have also been a formative event that shaped her views of authority, loyalty, and governance. As part of the Bonnycastle family, which had strong connections to the British Crown and the Loyalist cause, she would have been encouraged to uphold the ideals of loyalty to the British Empire, and the Rebellions would have reinforced this allegiance. The failure of the rebellions would have had a long-term impact on how the Bonnycastle family viewed their role in Upper Canada—strengthening their position within the loyalist establishment and further solidifying Catherine's ties to British colonial authority.

In conclusion, while Catherine Anne Bonnycastle would have been too young to fully understand the political intricacies of the Rebellions of 1837, the impact of the period on her childhood would have been significant. Her family's prominent role in Kingston's society, combined with the political unrest, would have shaped her experiences during these formative years. The tensions of the time, the disruptions to everyday life, and the role of her family within the colonial military would have all played a role in Catherine's early development and her understanding of the world around her.

CATHERINE ANNE BONNYCASTLE, at just 15 years old, passed away on June 27, 1845, in York (now Toronto), Ontario. Her untimely death at such a young age would have been a heartbreaking event for her family, particularly given her prominent background as the daughter of Sir Richard Bonnycastle and Frances Johnston Bonnycastle.

The Context of Her Passing

At the time of her death, Upper Canada (now Ontario) was still a growing colony, grappling with the legacy of the Rebellions of 1837 and the shifting dynamics of British rule. The region was slowly beginning to develop into a more stable society, with changes coming in the wake of the Rebellions, including shifts towards responsible government.

Catherine's death at 15 would have been deeply felt by those who knew her. As the daughter of a prominent military officer, she had likely been groomed to take on a public role in Upper Canadian society. Her untimely passing would have left an emotional void in the Bonnycastle family, as well as in the Kingston community, where she had connections.

Burial in St. Paul's Anglican Churchyard

Being buried in St. Paul's Anglican Churchyard in Kingston was a significant choice. Kingston was a major center of British influence in Upper Canada at the time, and St. Paul's Anglican Church had a special connection to the military and loyalist families in the region. It was a place of social and spiritual importance to those with ties to the British colonial establishment, and Catherine's burial there reflected both her family's status and the reverence with which she was likely regarded by her community.

St. Paul's Anglican Churchyard was not just a place of burial but also a testament to the enduring ties between British loyalists and the local community. Families like the Bonnycastles, who had been part of the loyalist establishment, would have considered this church a significant place for commemorating their ancestors. Catherine's grave, like many others in the churchyard, symbolized the legacy of those who had played an important part in the shaping of Upper Canada.

Catherine's Legacy

Though Catherine Anne Bonnycastle's life was tragically short, her family's legacy in Upper Canada lived on through her siblings and her father's continued service. Her death may have been a moment of personal loss for Sir Richard Bonnycastle, whose career continued to reflect the ongoing influence of British loyalists in the region.

Catherine's burial in Kingston, especially in such a notable Anglican churchyard, also speaks to the family's high social standing. The Bonnycastle family was influential in both military and civil affairs, and Catherine's premature death added another layer of sorrow to the history of the Bonnycastle name in the region. Her final resting place in St. Paul's Churchyard thus became a symbolic part of her family's ongoing presence in the colony's history.

Her brief life, set against the backdrop of Upper Canada's political and social evolution, may have been shaped by the same tensions that marked the lives of her peers—loyalist traditions, political upheaval, and the growing pains of a young colony. Catherine Anne Bonnycastle's passing at such a tender age was undoubtedly mourned by her family and those who had known her in York and Kingston, marking an early end to a promising life.

SIR. RICHARD HENRY BONNYCASTLE

SIR. RICHARD HENRY BONNYCASTLE[36]

In 1791, when Sir Richard Henry Bonnycastle was born in Woolwich, Kent, England, the world was on the cusp of significant political and industrial change. His birth occurred during the late Georgian era, which was marked by both great upheavals and important cultural developments.

The Context of 1791

Political and Social Landscape

Revolutionary Movements in Europe: The French Revolution, which began in 1789, had already begun to shake the foundations of Europe. By 1791, revolutionary fervor was spreading across the continent, and many European monarchies, including Britain, were alarmed by the ideas of liberty, equality, and fraternity. This period of political turbulence set the stage for the Napoleonic Wars, which would soon engulf much of Europe.

The Regency Era in Britain: In Britain, King George III was suffering from mental illness, which led to his son, the Prince of Wales, taking over the duties of the monarchy in what became known as the Regency period. The Regency was a time of extravagance, fashion, and cultural development, but it was also marked by political discontent and the fear of revolution.

British Empire and Colonialism: The British Empire was at its height, and Britain's influence around the world was vast. The colonial expansion continued across the Americas, Africa, Asia, and the Pacific, while tensions were rising in the American colonies, which had gained independence just over a decade earlier.

ECONOMIC AND TECHNOLOGICAL Context

The Industrial Revolution: The Industrial Revolution was beginning to reshape British society. In 1791, Britain was experiencing a period of rapid industrialization, particularly in the textile, iron, and coal industries. Mechanized production methods were transforming the economy, with factories beginning to replace traditional cottage industries. However, it was still early in the process, and many parts of the country, including rural Kent, had not yet fully embraced industrialization.

The Rise of the Middle Class: The early 19th century saw the rise of the middle class, a result of the economic boom brought on by industrialization, trade, and the wealth generated by the British Empire. Social mobility was becoming more possible for those who had the right skills, capital, or connections, a change that would significantly affect the lives of future generations, including Bonnycastle's.

FAMILY AND MILITARY Influence

British Army and Military Careers: In this period, many British men, particularly those of the landed gentry, pursued careers in the military. The British Army was engaged in several conflicts during this era, including the Napoleonic Wars, which began in 1803 and continued until 1815. This era also saw the growth of military service as a respectable career choice for younger sons of the upper classes, especially those who were not heirs to family estates.

The Navy and the Royal Military Academy: The Royal Navy was also expanding and becoming a dominant force in the world's oceans, and military academies, like the Royal Military Academy at Woolwich, where Richard Bonnycastle would later be associated, were training officers for the armed forces. The military played an integral part in British society, with a steady stream of talented men entering the Army and Navy, both of which would play key roles in the success of the British Empire.

DAILY LIFE IN 1791

Rural vs Urban Life: In the countryside, where Bonnycastle was born in Woolwich, life was still largely agrarian, with most people working the land. However, Woolwich was an industrial town and part of the larger metropolitan area of London, which had a bustling port and a growing urban population. Woolwich itself had long been associated with the British military, as it housed the Royal Arsenal, which would have influenced much of the town's character. The life of an upper-class child like Richard Bonnycastle would have been quite different, with access to education and an emphasis on social status and manners.

Family Life and Education: The Bonnycastle family, coming from a military background, would have likely placed a strong emphasis on discipline, education, and public service. Richard would have been taught at home by tutors or sent to a prestigious school, where he would have been trained in languages, mathematics, and military sciences.

CONCLUSION

The time of Richard Henry Bonnycastle's birth in 1791 was one of great change and transition in both Britain and the wider world. He was born into an era of political turmoil, social upheaval, and industrial transformation. The coming years would see Europe plunged into the Napoleonic Wars, which would have had a direct impact on his life and career. Bonnycastle would eventually contribute to the military and colonial history of Canada, but his early life was shaped by the broader trends of British imperialism, military tradition, and the early stirrings of industrial progress.

WHEN SIR RICHARD HENRY Bonnycastle was christened in Woolwich on October 30, 1791, the world around him was steeped in significant changes and events. This period, the final years of the 18th century, was marked by societal and political shifts, many of which would influence his life trajectory.

The Context of His Christening in Woolwich

1. The Political Climate

In Britain, the French Revolution (1789–1799) was causing deep anxiety in the aristocracy and monarchy. The ideals of liberty, fraternity, and equality were seen as a threat to the established social order, and many in Britain feared revolutionary fervor could spread across the English Channel.

The French Revolution directly impacted Britain's political stance and military strategies. The country was on high alert, and the possibility of conflict with France was very real. This military context may have influenced Bonnycastle's future path in the British Army, as his early life would be shaped by these tensions.

---

2. WOOLWICH AND ITS Significance

Woolwich, in Kent, was a key location for Britain's military activities. The Royal Arsenal was situated there, and it became a major center for the manufacturing of arms and military equipment. Woolwich was also home to the Royal Military Academy, where Bonnycastle would eventually pursue his career as a military officer. This strategic importance meant that Bonnycastle was born into an environment where military service and discipline were paramount.

---

3. RELIGIOUS CONTEXT

Bonnycastle's christening in Woolwich likely took place in a Church of England parish, in line with the Anglican faith that was dominant in Britain at the time. Baptism in the Anglican Church was an important rite of passage, signifying membership in the Church and community.

The late 18th century saw the Anglican Church strongly influencing British society, and those born into military or aristocratic families, like Bonnycastle, would often have strong ties to both the Church and the crown. These religious practices reinforced the social structure of the time, with an emphasis on duty, hierarchy, and family legacy.

---

4. FAMILY AND SOCIAL Influences

Richard Bonnycastle's family had ties to the British military, and his father's career would have further solidified his path. The Bonnycastle family, with its military and social connections, would have had high expectations for Richard, shaping his early education and future roles.

As a child born in a period of military unrest and an expanding British Empire, Bonnycastle would have been immersed in an environment where service to the Crown was both a duty and an honor.

Daily Life in 1791

The year 1791 was a time when much of Britain's elite class still lived in relative comfort. In Woolwich, the focus was on industry, military service, and trade. Life in an area like Woolwich would have been distinct from rural life, with a mix of military activity, industrial growth, and a growing population.

Bonnycastle, as a son of a family with military connections, would likely have received an education focused on preparation for a career in the armed forces. The environment he was born into would have provided him with the tools and opportunities to serve in the British Army, which at the time was a prestigious career choice.

CONCLUSION

Richard Henry Bonnycastle's christening in Woolwich on October 30, 1791, marked the beginning of a life that would unfold in the midst of a world on the brink of revolution, industrialization, and imperial expansion. Growing up in Woolwich, with its close ties to the British military, Bonnycastle was poised to contribute to Britain's colonial and military endeavors, particularly in Canada. His early life was shaped by the broader events of the 18th century, such as the political turmoil in Europe and the growing influence of the British Empire across the world.

WHEN SIR RICHARD HENRY Bonnycastle was four years old, in 1795, Dr. Edward Jenner introduced the first successful smallpox vaccination. This was a revolutionary moment in medical history, marking the beginning of the end for a disease that had killed millions over centuries.

Context of Jenner's Discovery

1. The Situation with Smallpox

Smallpox had been one of the deadliest diseases in history, spreading across continents and leaving devastating effects on populations. It caused severe fever, disfigurement, and death in many of its victims.

In the late 18th century, smallpox was still rampant in many parts of the world, including Britain. During this period, smallpox was particularly dangerous, as there was no effective cure or method to prevent it.

---

2. JENNER'S DISCOVERY

Dr. Edward Jenner, a British physician, is credited with developing the first successful smallpox vaccine in 1796. His method involved inoculating a person with cowpox, a much milder disease, which provided immunity to smallpox. Jenner's discovery came from observing that milkmaids who had contracted cowpox seemed to be immune to smallpox.

Jenner conducted a famous experiment in May 1796 by inoculating a young boy, James Phipps, with material from a cowpox sore and later exposing him to smallpox. The boy did not develop smallpox, proving that the cowpox inoculation was effective in providing immunity.

---

3. THE IMPACT

Jenner's work was revolutionary, and while it was initially met with skepticism, it eventually became widely accepted as the method to prevent smallpox. Over the following decades, vaccination programs were implemented globally, and smallpox eventually became the first disease to be eradicated by vaccination in 1980.

For someone like Sir Richard Henry Bonnycastle, born in 1791, this moment marked the beginning of a new era in medicine. By the time he reached adulthood, the use of vaccines would become a crucial part of public health, and Jenner's work would lay the foundation for the development of modern immunology.

Impact on Bonnycastle's Lifetime

Though Bonnycastle would not have been directly affected by the smallpox vaccination as a child, as it was not immediately widespread, the discovery would have had long-term effects on the society he lived in. Throughout his life, he would witness the growing acceptance and development of vaccines as a cornerstone of public health.

By the time Bonnycastle reached adulthood and moved to Canada, Jenner's work would have laid the groundwork for future medical advancements, including the use of vaccination in preventing other diseases. This would also have been significant in the context of British colonial life, where disease and health were central to the survival of settlers and soldiers. Bonnycastle, as a soldier and later as a settler, would have been part of a world that increasingly embraced the value of vaccination to protect populations from deadly diseases.

WHEN SIR RICHARD HENRY Bonnycastle was 15 years old, in 1806, Robert Fulton launched the first commercially successful steamboat, the Clermont. This was a transformative moment in transportation history.

Context of the Steamboat's Development

1. Robert Fulton's Innovation

Robert Fulton, an American engineer and inventor, is most famously known for the Clermont, a steamboat that revolutionized river travel in the early 19th century. In 1807, the Clermont made its maiden voyage along the Hudson River between New York City and Albany, marking the first successful demonstration of a steamboat for commercial purposes.

Fulton's steamboat had a steam engine designed by James Watt and Matthew Boulton. It was able to travel at an average speed of about 5 miles per hour (8 kilometers per hour), which was faster than any sailing vessel at the time. This was a major achievement, as prior attempts at steam-powered boats had largely failed or were impractical.

2. THE IMPACT ON TRANSPORTATION

The success of the Clermont made steamboats a viable mode of transportation for both passengers and freight. Prior to this, river travel had been dependent on wind or manual power, limiting the speed and efficiency of boats. Fulton's steamboat dramatically improved the efficiency of transportation, reducing travel time and boosting trade and commerce along rivers.

The success of the steamboat also opened the door for the development of steamships, which would later revolutionize ocean travel and global trade. It laid the foundation for the expansion of steam-powered navigation, which would become critical for economic growth and the development of new industries.

Bonnycastle's Life at the Time

At the age of 15 in 1806, Bonnycastle was likely beginning to mature as a young man, and the rapid advancements in technology and industry during this period would have influenced his worldview. By this time, the Industrial Revolution was already making waves in Britain, and innovations such as steam-powered engines would eventually reach Canada and the broader North American continent.

Bonnycastle, being born in Woolwich, a site known for its military history and proximity to the technological developments of Britain, would have been in an environment where the effects of industrial and technological innovations were starting to be felt. While he may not have been directly involved with the maritime or steam-powered industries, the success of Fulton's steamboat would have contributed to the general sense of progress and change in transportation, which was central to the global economic expansion of the time.

The growth of steam-powered travel would later influence Bonnycastle's own career, especially as he moved into the military and colonial life in Canada, where efficient transportation would become increasingly important for trade, settlement, and military logistics. By the time Bonnycastle established himself in Canada, steamships would have become critical for connecting the provinces and territories, contributing to the expansion of the British Empire's influence in North America.

WHEN SIR RICHARD HENRY Bonnycastle married Lady Frances Johnstone on August 6, 1812, at the age of 20, it was during a period of significant political, military, and social change in Britain and its colonies.

The Historical Context of 1812

1. The Napoleonic Wars

The Napoleonic Wars (1803–1815) were ongoing at the time of their marriage. Britain was deeply involved in conflict with Napoleon Bonaparte's France. The wars had major economic and military consequences, and Britain's focus was on maintaining its global influence, particularly through naval superiority. The wars would continue to shape British politics and society for years to come.

Bonnycastle, coming from a military family, would have been deeply aware of the wars' implications. As a young officer in the British Army, he would likely have been influenced by the patriotic fervor and the opportunities that came with military service during this time.

---

2. THE WAR OF 1812

The War of 1812 between the United States and Britain was also unfolding around the time of Bonnycastle's marriage. The conflict was rooted in a variety of causes, including trade restrictions, the impressment of American sailors into the British navy, and American expansionist desires. Bonnycastle, who later became involved in military service in Canada, would be particularly affected by this war. It had a profound impact on the British colonies in North America, where Bonnycastle would serve.

---

3. SOCIAL AND MARRIAGE Norms

At the time, marriages among the British upper classes were often arranged or influenced by family connections, wealth, and social standing. Bonnycastle's marriage to Lady Frances Johnstone, likely a woman of significant social rank, would have been consistent with these norms. Frances was the daughter of Sir John Johnstone, a Scottish nobleman.

The marriage was not only a personal union but also a strategic alliance, helping strengthen Bonnycastle's ties to the British aristocracy and giving him greater social influence. As a young officer in the army, Bonnycastle would have been seeking to establish himself, and a well-connected marriage could enhance his career prospects.

---

4. THE INFLUENCE OF Edinburgh

The city of Edinburgh in 1812 was a thriving intellectual and cultural hub, known for its universities, its role in the Scottish Enlightenment, and its political significance in Britain. The Bonnycastles' marriage in this vibrant city reflects the social prominence of both families. Edinburgh was a center of political and military thought, and Bonnycastle would have been in the midst of a society steeped in the era's ideas about liberty, power, and the importance of military service.

---

5. BONNYCASTLE'S MILITARY Career

Bonnycastle was a young officer at the time of his marriage. He would go on to have a distinguished career in the Royal Engineers and later as a military officer in Canada. His marriage to Frances could have strengthened his ties to the British Army and positioned him for future advancement. Bonnycastle's service in Canada, particularly during the War of 1812, would become a key part of his career.

Life After Marriage

Following their marriage, Bonnycastle and Lady Frances Johnstone would have experienced the challenges of military life during the Napoleonic Wars and the turbulent years of the War of 1812. Their union would also be shaped by the growing imperial presence of Britain in North America, which would lead to Bonnycastle's eventual relocation to Canada, where he became a prominent figure.

The early years of their marriage would have been marked by Bonnycastle's military service, his travels, and his eventual establishment in Canada, where he would play a crucial role in the development of Canadian military infrastructure.

WHEN SIR RICHARD HENRY Bonnycastle was 21 years old, his son, Henry William John Bonnycastle, was born on July 24, 1813, in Cumberland, England. This was a time of intense political and military activity for Bonnycastle, as well as a key moment in his personal life.

The Historical Context of 1813

1. The Napoleonic Wars (1803–1815)

The Napoleonic Wars were still raging across Europe in 1813, and the British Empire was fully engaged in the conflict. For someone like Bonnycastle, who was part of the British military establishment, these years were crucial. Bonnycastle's career was directly shaped by these wars, and by 1813, he would have been gaining valuable military experience in preparation for the war's eventual conclusion in 1815.

---

2. THE WAR OF 1812

The War of 1812 between Britain and the United States was another key conflict for Bonnycastle at this time. Although Bonnycastle was in England when his son was born, the war would soon involve him directly. His future military service in Canada—where the majority of the fighting between British forces and American troops occurred—was a critical part of his career. The British victory in Canada during the War of 1812 would be part of his legacy, and his experience would influence his later work in North America.

---

3. THE BATTLE OF LEIPZIG (October 1813)

The year 1813 also saw one of the major turning points of the Napoleonic Wars, the Battle of Leipzig (also known as the Battle of Nations). It was a major defeat for Napoleon, and it set the stage for his eventual downfall. This pivotal event would have impacted the global political landscape, shaping the future of the British Empire, as well as Bonnycastle's career trajectory.

Bonnycastle's Life in 1813

Personal Life: The birth of Henry William John Bonnycastle marked a major milestone in Bonnycastle's personal life. As a young man, Bonnycastle would have been balancing the pressures of his military career and the responsibilities of fatherhood. He had recently married Lady Frances Johnstone in 1812, and their son's birth in 1813 solidified their family life. This period of his life was likely one of growth, both professionally and personally, as he would have seen the arrival of his first child while also establishing himself as an officer in the British Army.

Military Service: At the time, Bonnycastle was likely engaged in military training and preparation for future assignments. His role in the Royal Engineers was important, especially in the context of the growing tensions between Britain and the United States. Bonnycastle's future service would take him to Canada, where his contributions during the War of 1812 would eventually earn him recognition.

LIFE IN CUMBERLAND, England

Cumberland in 1813: Cumberland in 1813 was a rural area, far from the bustling cities like London or Edinburgh. However, it had a strong connection to the British military, as the north of England had long been home to several regiments and military personnel. Cumberland was also known for its scenic landscapes and the influence of the Industrial Revolution, though it was still more rural than industrialized. Life here in the early 19th century would have been relatively quiet compared to the larger centers of activity, but it was still deeply impacted by the social, political, and military events of the time.

The Bonnycastle Family: Bonnycastle's family, with his wife Frances, would likely have spent much of this time in the relatively peaceful English countryside, even though their lives were influenced by the distant rumblings of war. Frances' noble background likely afforded them a certain level of comfort and social standing. The birth of their son Henry would have been a joyous occasion, and Bonnycastle would have felt the weight of fatherhood while preparing for the future military responsibilities that awaited him in Canada.

HENRY WILLIAM JOHN Bonnycastle's Early Years

Henry William John Bonnycastle was born into a world shaped by British imperial power and military conflict. His father, Sir Richard Bonnycastle, would have been a source of both influence and inspiration for him, as Bonnycastle's military career was set to take off over the coming years. Henry's early years would have been influenced by the grand narrative of British imperial expansion and the military's role in shaping the future of the British Empire, particularly in North America.

IN SUM, HENRY WILLIAM John Bonnycastle's birth in 1813 symbolized a moment of growth for Sir Richard Bonnycastle as both a soldier and a father, amidst a world of conflict and change that would define the early 19th century.

WHEN SIR RICHARD HENRY Bonnycastle was 25 years old, his daughter, Jane Hume Bonnycastle, was born in France on June 10, 1817. This period marked a significant time in Bonnycastle's life, both personally and professionally.

The Historical Context of 1817

1. Post-Napoleonic Era (1815 Onwards):

By 1817, the Napoleonic Wars had ended with Napoleon's defeat at Waterloo in 1815. Europe was transitioning into a period of peace after nearly two decades of constant warfare. The Congress of Vienna (1814-1815) had reshaped the political landscape, aiming to restore stability and maintain the balance of power in Europe. Sir Richard Bonnycastle, as an officer in the British military, would have been adjusting to the post-war environment, with many former soldiers either returning to civilian life or moving into new roles, particularly within the British Empire.

---

2. THE RISE OF THE British Empire:

The British Empire continued to expand during this time, with British interests in North America, the Caribbean, and Asia continuing to grow. For Bonnycastle, this meant that the opportunities for service in various imperial ventures would continue to shape his career. His future service in Canada and subsequent military engagements in the colonies were part of the broader imperial ambitions of the British government.

---

3. THE INDUSTRIAL REVOLUTION:

The Industrial Revolution was in full swing by 1817. This had profound effects on Britain and its colonies, with rapid advancements in manufacturing, transportation (such as the steam engine), and communication. While Sir Richard Bonnycastle's military career would not be directly linked to these industrial changes, they would have influenced the broader economy and imperial strategies of the time.

---

4. FRENCH POLITICAL Landscape:

Since Jane Hume Bonnycastle was born in France in 1817, it's important to note the political context in which the Bonnycastle family lived. In 1817, France was under the Bourbon Restoration, with Louis XVIII on the throne. The monarchy had been restored after Napoleon's fall, but France was still grappling with the effects of the revolution and the Napoleonic era. Bonnycastle's time in France would likely have been during a period of relative peace, but France was still recovering from the tumultuous events of the late 18th and early 19th centuries.

Sir Richard Bonnycastle's Personal Life in 1817

Fatherhood: The birth of his daughter Jane Hume Bonnycastle marked a new chapter in Bonnycastle's personal life. As a young father, Bonnycastle would have been adjusting to the demands of family life while continuing to advance in his military career. The choice to have his daughter born in France may have been related to his military service or personal circumstances at the time. The Bonnycastle family likely enjoyed a certain level of social standing and privilege, given Sir Richard's military position and his marriage to Lady Frances Johnstone.

Life in France: Living in France during this time would have been interesting for Bonnycastle. Despite the political changes, France was still a major European cultural and intellectual hub. The Bonnycastle family would have been part of the cosmopolitan atmosphere of post-revolutionary France, though Bonnycastle's exact reasons for being in France are not clear. It could have been related to his military duties, as many British officers were stationed in European capitals following the Napoleonic Wars, or it could have been for personal reasons.

THE BONNYCASTLE FAMILY in France

The Bonnycastle family likely spent time in an environment that was politically complex and culturally rich. For young Jane Hume Bonnycastle, the family's time in France would have exposed her to a unique set of cultural influences that could have shaped her upbringing. The connection to the Hume name (likely through her mother, Lady Frances Johnstone) suggests a family with noble Scottish roots, and this may have played a role in the family's social standing in both England and France.

THE SIGNIFICANCE OF Jane Hume Bonnycastle's Birth

Jane Hume Bonnycastle's birth in France in 1817 marked an important moment for the Bonnycastle family. While Sir Richard was already an established figure in the British military, the arrival of a daughter added to the personal legacy he was building. It also indicated the family's international mobility and connections to both British and European aristocracy. The child's upbringing in such a politically dynamic period would be notable, given the ongoing changes in Europe after the fall of Napoleon.

CONCLUSION

The year 1817 was a time of significant change in Europe and for the Bonnycastle family. For Sir Richard Henry Bonnycastle, it was a period of adjustment to post-war life, both personally as a father and professionally as a military officer. The birth of his daughter Jane Hume Bonnycastle in France added a new chapter to his personal life while highlighting the family's international ties and influence. This moment in history would shape Jane's early years and her eventual role in the Bonnycastle family legacy.

WHEN SIR RICHARD HENRY Bonnycastle was 27 years old, his son John Bonnycastle was born in Island Bridge, County Dublin, Ireland, on June 16, 1819. Tragically, John passed away just a few months later, on September 19, 1819.

Historical Context of 1819

1. Post-War Britain:

In 1819, Europe was still recovering from the aftermath of the Napoleonic Wars, which had significantly impacted the continent. Sir Richard Bonnycastle, having served in the British military during these wars, would have been adjusting to a life of relative peace. However, the social and political climates in both Britain and Ireland remained charged during this time, particularly in Ireland, where the effects of British rule were a source of considerable tension.

---

2. IRELAND IN 1819:

In Ireland, the year 1819 was part of a difficult period in Irish history, marked by economic hardship, political unrest, and dissatisfaction with British rule. This period saw the rise of various political movements, including those seeking Irish independence and reform, though it would not be until later in the century that these movements gained substantial traction.

Island Bridge in Dublin, where John Bonnycastle was born, was a notable area located close to the River Liffey, and at the time, it was a mix of residential and industrial areas. The Bonnycastle family's presence in Dublin would have exposed them to the political and social dynamics in one of the most important cities in the British Isles. This would likely have been a time of personal and family adjustment for Sir Richard, balancing his military duties with family life.

---

3. INFANT MORTALITY:

The death of John Bonnycastle at just a few months old was a sad reality of the time. Infant mortality was tragically common in the early 19th century due to a combination of factors including disease, malnutrition, and limited medical care. This personal loss would have deeply affected Sir Richard and his wife, Lady Frances Johnstone, as the death of an infant was often a sorrowful experience for many families of the period.

The Bonnycastle Family's Loss

The birth and subsequent death of John Bonnycastle was a heartbreaking event for the Bonnycastle family. For Sir Richard, it represented not only the loss of a son but also a reflection of the fragility of life during that period. It is important to note that during the early 19th century, infant mortality rates were significantly high, and families often experienced multiple child deaths. The short life of John Bonnycastle was sadly not uncommon, but it was a devastating loss nonetheless.

Lady Frances Johnstone, Sir Richard's wife, would have had to navigate the grief of losing a young child while raising the family, particularly with their other children, including Jane Hume Bonnycastle. Losing a child at such a young age was not only an emotional burden but also a reminder of the challenges families faced in this era.

CONCLUSION

The year 1819 marked both a time of personal joy and deep sorrow for Sir Richard Henry Bonnycastle and his family. While the birth of John Bonnycastle in Ireland was a moment of hope, his passing just a few months later underscored the fragility of life in the early 19th century, particularly for families dealing with infant mortality. The Bonnycastle family's experience during this period reflects the broader social and historical realities of the time.

WHEN SIR RICHARD HENRY Bonnycastle was 29 years old, his son Charles Bonnycastle was born in Dublin, County Dublin, Ireland, on August 30, 1821. Sadly, Charles passed away just a few months later, on January 25, 1822.

Historical Context of 1821-1822

1. The Early 1820s:

The period when Charles Bonnycastle was born was marked by political and social unrest in Ireland. Following the end of the Napoleonic Wars, Europe was entering a phase of economic instability, and in Ireland, the effects of British colonial rule were still deeply felt. There were frequent calls for reform and greater autonomy, particularly from Irish nationalists and those advocating for better conditions for the Irish peasantry.

---

2. INFANT MORTALITY and Family Life:

The death of Charles Bonnycastle at such a young age reflects the high infant mortality rates of the time. Between disease, malnutrition, and limited medical advancements, many families faced the sorrow of losing children before they reached adulthood. For Sir Richard and his wife, Lady Frances Johnstone, this would have been another devastating loss. The early 19th century was an especially difficult time for families in terms of health, as infant mortality was prevalent due to poor sanitation and the lack of modern medical practices.

---

3. LIFE IN DUBLIN:

Dublin, during this period, was a bustling city with both the cultural vibrancy of Ireland's capital and the tensions of political and social unrest. Dublin was home to many significant historical events during the early 19th century. However, for the Bonnycastle family, Charles

Bonnycastle's death in Ireland would have been an intensely personal tragedy. The city, while a center of intellectual and social life, was not immune to the difficulties that families faced at the time, particularly concerning public health and the hardships associated with raising children.

---

4. IMPACT ON SIR RICHARD Bonnycastle:

For Sir Richard Bonnycastle, a British army officer with significant military experience, the loss of two children in his relatively young family would have been a profound emotional blow. Though he was accustomed to the hardships of military life, such personal loss would have been a constant sorrow for him and his wife. Losing Charles, just as they had lost John two years earlier, may have made him feel the fragility of life more keenly.

The Bonnycastle Family's Loss

The death of Charles Bonnycastle in 1822 would have been a sorrowful experience for the family. Losing two children at such a young age—John in 1819 and Charles in 1822—would likely have weighed heavily on Sir Richard and Lady Frances, despite the public life Sir Richard led as a military officer. For many families of this time, the loss of children was tragically common, though no less painful.

The experience of losing children was an unfortunate reality for many families in early 19th-century Ireland and the British Empire, especially in the wake of the Napoleonic Wars. For Sir Richard, the death of his son Charles would have been yet another reminder of the challenges faced by families during that period, particularly regarding the vulnerabilities of young children.

CONCLUSION

The birth and subsequent death of Charles Bonnycastle in 1821-1822 reflects a broader historical context in which families struggled with high infant mortality rates, compounded by the social and political challenges of the early 19th century. For Sir Richard Henry Bonnycastle, this personal loss would have been another devastating chapter in the family's history, alongside the earlier loss of John. As a military man, he would have seen the larger struggles of the world but no doubt felt the emotional toll of his personal losses deeply. This era was one of great social and political change, but it was also one marked by sorrow and hardship for many families like the Bonnycastles.

WHEN SIR RICHARD HENRY Bonnycastle was 30 years old, his son Francis Bonnycastle was born on June 27, 1822, in Island Bridge, County Dublin, Ireland.

Historical Context of 1822

1. Political Landscape:

The year 1822 was a time of growing unrest and political change in Ireland. The Irish population, particularly in urban centers like Dublin, was becoming increasingly discontent with British rule, leading to the rise of Irish nationalist movements. This was just a few years after the end of the Irish Rebellion of 1798, and tensions between the Irish populace and British authorities remained high.

In 1822, Ireland was still under the influence of Anglo-Irish rule, with English laws and policies affecting the daily lives of the Irish. The Act of Union of 1801 had created the United Kingdom of Great Britain and Ireland, but there was a strong sense of national identity among many Irish people, leading to calls for reforms and greater self-governance.

---

2. LIFE IN DUBLIN:

Dublin in the early 1820s was a bustling city, experiencing a mix of growth and difficulty. The Napoleonic Wars had ended, but their effects were still felt in terms of economic instability, social upheaval, and a sense of unrest among the Irish population.

The urbanization of Dublin was also evident as the city grew to accommodate the increasing population. Yet, despite the bustling city life, the living conditions for many, especially the poor and working classes, were often poor and overcrowded, with rampant disease and high infant mortality.

---

3. THE BONNYCASTLE Family:

The birth of Francis Bonnycastle in 1822 was likely a hopeful moment for Sir Richard Henry Bonnycastle and his wife, Lady Frances Johnstone, following the tragic deaths of their earlier children, John (1819) and Charles (1822). After enduring such sorrow, the birth of a new child could have brought a renewed sense of joy and optimism for the Bonnycastle family.

Francis' birth in Island Bridge further cements the Bonnycastle family's deep ties to Dublin, which was both an important cultural and political center at the time. Island Bridge was located near the center of the city, close to many significant landmarks, and the area was becoming more developed during this period.

---

4. THE MILITARY CONTEXT:

Sir Richard Henry Bonnycastle was deeply entrenched in military life, serving as an officer in the British army and participating in several important military campaigns. His life was closely tied to the Empire's global military operations, and his family life, including the birth of Francis, was lived under the shadow of military duty.

Given his military background, Sir Richard would have been familiar with the challenges faced by families of servicemen—separation, uncertainty, and the constant movement tied to military life. However, the birth of a son may have given him a sense of continuity, particularly after experiencing the losses of John and Charles.

---

5. CHILDBIRTH AND FAMILY Life in Early 19th Century Ireland:

The birth of Francis Bonnycastle also reflects the norms of the time, when families in the upper classes often had multiple children. However, high infant mortality rates remained a stark reality, and the Bonnycastle family had already experienced the heartbreak of losing two children in the early 1820s. This made Francis' survival even more precious.

In 1822, childbirth was still a dangerous undertaking, even for women in the more privileged classes. The lack of modern medical practices and the risks of diseases such as puerperal fever meant that many families faced the possibility of losing mothers or infants during childbirth.

Conclusion

The birth of Francis Bonnycastle in 1822 brought a moment of joy to the Bonnycastle family, marking a new chapter for Sir Richard Henry Bonnycastle and his wife, Lady Frances Johnstone. It was a time of political change and social unrest in Ireland, with growing calls for Irish self-rule and increased tensions between the Irish and the British. For the Bonnycastle family, the arrival of Francis represented hope and continuity after the loss of two earlier children. It was also a reminder of the precariousness of life during this era, when disease and high infant mortality were common challenges faced by families.

WHEN SIR RICHARD HENRY Bonnycastle was 32 years old, his daughter Charlotte Bonnycastle was born on May 21, 1824.

Context of 1824

1. Political and Social Landscape:

In 1824, the political atmosphere in Ireland remained tense, with continued calls for Irish reform, though the Catholic Emancipation Act had been passed in 1829, allowing Catholics to hold public office. The events of the 1820s laid the groundwork for future movements advocating for Irish rights and independence, although the rebellion in 1837 would still be a decade away.

For Dublin, the 1820s marked a period of urban expansion, but the city was still grappling with issues of poverty, disease, and overcrowding, particularly in the poorer sections of the city. Charlotte's birth occurred amid a society that was slowly adjusting to the post-war world but still struggling with the impacts of the Napoleonic Wars on the economy and class divisions.

---

2. MILITARY CONTEXT:

Sir Richard Henry Bonnycastle, having been involved in the British military, may have been stationed at the time in Ireland or elsewhere in the Empire. As a military officer, his life would have been defined by duty and deployment, with the threat of military conflict ever-present.

In 1824, Bonnycastle would have been actively involved in the British military infrastructure and may have witnessed developments in military technology, such as the increasing use of steam-powered ships in the Royal Navy and the advancements in artillery.

---

3. FAMILY LIFE:

The birth of Charlotte would have been another significant event for the Bonnycastle family. After the tragic deaths of his sons John and Charles, the birth of a daughter brought a sense of renewal and joy to the family. Given the military and aristocratic nature of the Bonnycastle family, Charlotte's birth would likely have been celebrated in an upper-class, traditional manner, though the challenges of childbirth still loomed.

Sir Richard had already experienced the loss of two children in the early 1820s, so Charlotte's birth in 1824 would have brought hope that the family could now focus on providing a stable future for their surviving children.

---

4. CULTURAL AND TECHNOLOGICAL Landscape:

The early 1820s were a time of scientific exploration and cultural shifts. The Romantic Era in literature and art was reaching its peak, with figures such as Lord Byron and Percy Bysshe Shelley influencing the intellectual currents of the time.

In terms of technology, steam engines were becoming more common, particularly in transportation. The development of the steam-powered locomotive and steamships represented a major leap forward in human mobility, which would have greatly impacted British and Irish trade, communication, and warfare in the years that followed.

Charlotte's birth came at a time when education and scientific advancement were becoming more accessible, even though the upper classes continued to enjoy privileges such as private tutors and exclusive schooling for their children.

---

5. LIVING CONDITIONS:

For Sir Richard's family, the year 1824 likely saw Charlotte born into relative comfort compared to the general population, with access to healthcare, education, and a stable home environment. However, even wealthy families were not immune to the dangers of disease and the high rates of infant mortality that plagued many parts of the world during the early 19th century.

As a member of the British Army and a man of status, Sir Richard would have likely been able to afford a comfortable lifestyle for his family. However, even within the aristocracy, families still had to contend with the uncertainties of life, particularly in the wake of the early deaths of his earlier children.

Conclusion

The birth of Charlotte Bonnycastle in 1824 was a significant moment in the Bonnycastle family's life, offering hope and renewal after the losses they had endured. Sir Richard Henry Bonnycastle, as a military officer, would have experienced the political and social shifts of the time, including the ongoing tensions in Ireland and the post-war realities of the British Empire. In a world of rapid technological progress and cultural change, Charlotte's arrival symbolized both a personal triumph for the family and the continuation of the Bonnycastle legacy.

WHEN SIR RICHARD HENRY Bonnycastle was 32 years old, his son William Henry John Bonnycastle passed away on August 16, 1824, in Kent, England. This was a devastating event for the Bonnycastle family, particularly for Sir Richard and his wife, Lady Frances Johnston.

Context of 1824

1. Personal Tragedy:

The death of William Henry John, at such a young age, would have been particularly sorrowful for the Bonnycastle family. Having already experienced the loss of John and Charles, this would have been another heavy blow to the family. The high infant and child mortality rates during the period made it all the more painful for families like the Bonnycastles, who had the resources to ensure good healthcare but were not immune to the tragic fragility of life.

As a military officer, Sir Richard might have been away or engaged in his duties during this time, possibly compounding the emotional strain on his family. While military life provided a certain structure and honor, it also distanced men like Sir Richard from their families at critical moments.

---

2. FAMILY AND EMOTIONAL Impact:

The death of William Henry John would have weighed heavily on Frances Johnston Bonnycastle, as mothers in the 19th century often endured the brunt of child-rearing and were typically more affected by the loss of children. For both Frances and Richard, the repeated tragedies of child loss would have likely brought about a sense of grief, leaving a profound mark on their personal lives.

This loss likely impacted the Bonnycastle family dynamic, possibly making them even more protective of their surviving children. The sense of fragility of life, especially with the death of another son, would have drawn the family closer, albeit under the shadow of grief.

---

3. SOCIETAL CONTEXT:

In 1824, England was still reeling from the consequences of the Napoleonic Wars, which had ended just a few years earlier. The population was experiencing some recovery, but many families still faced hardships. Advances in medicine were occurring, but they had not yet reached the level where childhood diseases could be reliably treated.

The upper class, including families like the Bonnycastles, had better access to resources, but death in the family, especially that of a child, was still a common and tragic occurrence. The social structure remained largely hierarchical, and family tragedies were handled with a certain stoicism in public, though in private they were deeply affecting.

4. MILITARY AND HISTORICAL Context:

Sir Richard would have still been in his military career in 1824 and perhaps engaged in administrative or strategic duties as part of the British Army. Given the post-Napoleonic period, the British military was undergoing a phase of reorganization and had begun focusing more on maintaining imperial control and defending British interests globally. However, for officers like Sir Richard, personal life often remained somewhat separated from their military careers.

Conclusion

The death of William Henry John Bonnycastle in 1824, when Sir Richard was 32 years old, marked yet another personal tragedy for the family. The Bonnycastle family, already familiar with the grief of losing children, would have been deeply affected by this loss. For Sir Richard, a soldier dedicated to his country, and Lady Frances, who had already endured the deaths of multiple children, this event would have been a heart-wrenching chapter in their lives, influencing the course of their family's history.

WHEN SIR RICHARD HENRY Bonnycastle was 33 years old, his son Murray Bonnycastle was born on July 9, 1825, in Plumstead, England.

Context of 1825

1. Personal Joy:

The birth of Murray in 1825 would have been a source of joy and hope for Sir Richard and Lady Frances Johnston Bonnycastle, especially after the sorrow of losing several children in earlier years. His arrival likely brought a sense of renewal to the family and may have helped alleviate some of the grief from the deaths of their other children, such as William Henry John, Charles, and John.

Having a son during this time would have been particularly meaningful, as sons often carried on the family name, legacy, and responsibilities, especially in military families. Murray's birth would have likely been seen as a positive development for Sir Richard, reinforcing his role as a father and patriarch.

---

2. THE FAMILY DYNAMIC:

The Bonnycastle family, despite its earlier losses, was now growing with Murray joining his siblings, including Charlotte (born in 1824) and Francis (born in 1822). As Sir Richard was well-established in his military career, the birth of Murray may have been a reason for the family to celebrate during a time when personal and national issues were still heavy with the aftereffects of the Napoleonic Wars.

For Lady Frances, Murray's birth likely brought renewed joy and hope for the future, as she had endured much pain with the loss of multiple children. The addition of a new son would have strengthened her position within the family as the mother of the next generation.

---

3. SOCIETAL CONTEXT:

In 1825, England was beginning to experience significant industrial and social change. The Industrial Revolution was altering the fabric of society, bringing economic progress and change to the family structures of the time. The Bonnycastles, as part of the British military elite, would have been somewhat insulated from the broader societal upheavals but would have still been influenced by the changing times, especially in terms of the growing emphasis on technological and military advancements.

For a military family like the Bonnycastles, Murray's birth would have had significance in ensuring the continuity of the family name and legacy within an environment of shifting political and industrial realities.

---

4. MILITARY CONTEXT:

Sir Richard had likely just returned to a more stable routine following the end of the Napoleonic Wars. As a soldier, he would have been transitioning from wartime engagements to peacetime duties, and his family would have been a stabilizing force in his life.

Murray's birth would have reinforced Sir Richard's connection to his heritage as a British officer, emphasizing the importance of maintaining family traditions, especially in light of his earlier responsibilities in the military. The military life, often fraught with personal sacrifice, was made all the more poignant by the birth of another son.

---

5. PLUMSTEAD:

Plumstead, located in Greater London, was an area with a military presence due to its proximity to London and military establishments. Sir Richard may have been stationed there or had connections with local military operations. The birth of Murray in Plumstead would place the family within a broader military and social context that was undergoing significant transformation during the early 19th century.

Conclusion

The birth of Murray Bonnycastle in 1825, when Sir Richard Henry Bonnycastle was 33 years old, marked a period of personal renewal and joy for the family after several tragic losses. It provided hope for the future and was a continuation of the family legacy within a rapidly changing England. For Sir Richard and Lady Frances, Murray's birth would have been a symbol of new beginnings, signaling the possibility of a more prosperous and stable family life amidst the aftermath of war and loss.

WHEN SIR RICHARD HENRY Bonnycastle was 34 years old, in 1826, the invention of matches was a significant event in the advancement of everyday life.

The invention of the modern match is attributed to John Walker, an English chemist. In 1826, Walker accidentally discovered how to ignite a chemical mixture on a rough surface, leading to the creation of the first friction match. He initially called them "congress fire," and they were sold in small boxes. These early matches were not as convenient as today's matches—they had to be struck on a specific surface, and they often emitted a strong odor and smoke.

The Context of 1826

1. Technological Innovation:

The invention of the match in 1826 marked a major advancement in the everyday life of people in Europe and beyond. Before matches, people used flint and steel or slow-burning tinder to create fire, a process that was much slower, less reliable, and required special tools. The introduction of matches would have had a profound effect on everyday living, making it easier to light stoves, fireplaces, and candles—especially in military and household contexts.

---

2. LIFE IN 1826:

For Sir Richard Bonnycastle, a 34-year-old military officer, the invention of matches would have been a significant improvement in the ease and safety of lighting fires, particularly in his personal and military life. Matches would eventually find use in both everyday life and military settings—lighting fires for cooking, heating, and signaling would become more efficient.

The military context in particular would have been impacted, as soldiers could carry matches instead of relying on more cumbersome fire-starting methods. This development could have even influenced military logistics, making it easier for troops to maintain warmth and light during campaigns or garrisons.

---

3. INDUSTRIAL REVOLUTION:

The year 1826 was during the Industrial Revolution, a time of rapid technological and societal change. The creation of the match was just one of many innovations that helped to shape the modern world. This era saw advancements in machinery, transportation (like steamships and railways), and manufacturing processes. The match was a simple yet important example of how new technologies improved the daily lives of people, making tasks faster and more convenient.

CONCLUSION:

In 1826, when Sir Richard Henry Bonnycastle was 34, the invention of the match was a technological milestone that would revolutionize how people started fires in everyday life. As a military officer and a member of British society, Sir Richard would have witnessed this change firsthand, appreciating its impact on both personal convenience and military functionality. The match, alongside other advancements of the Industrial Revolution, marked the beginning of a new age of convenience and progress in both civilian and military spheres.

AT 35 YEARS OLD, IN 1826, Sir Richard Henry Bonnycastle faced the heartbreaking loss of his son Francis in Ontario, Canada, on November 28, 1826. This tragic event would have been deeply emotional for Sir Richard and his wife, Frances Johnston.

During this period, Ontario was still part of Upper Canada and was undergoing significant changes as the British colonial presence in North America continued to evolve. The death of a child, particularly so far from home, in a colony that was still in the early stages of development, would have likely had profound personal and emotional ramifications for Sir Richard and his family.

Context in 1826:

1. Life in Ontario in 1826:

In 1826, Upper Canada (modern-day Ontario) was in the midst of expanding its settlements and infrastructure, though it was still a largely rural and frontier society. Many of the challenges faced by residents included isolation, limited medical care, and the struggles of pioneering a new life in the harsh conditions of the Canadian wilderness. Disease, such as smallpox, tuberculosis, and cholera, were common and could take the lives of many, including children.

---

2. THE BONNYCASTLE Family's Situation:

Francis' death, especially at such a young age, would have been a devastating blow to Sir Richard and his wife, Frances. Given Sir Richard's military background, he may have been stationed or involved in some capacity with the British colonial administration in Upper Canada during that time, which might have meant being away from his family at times. The death of their son, far from their home in England, could have compounded feelings of grief, loss, and perhaps even isolation, as communication and travel between Upper Canada and England would have been slow and difficult.

---

3. BRITISH COLONIAL Presence in Canada:

As a British officer, Sir Richard was likely aware of the complexities of life in the colonies. Upper Canada was home to many military and civilian families who had made the journey from Britain, including members of the Royal Engineers, who were involved in fortification and infrastructure projects. However, the loss of a child in such an environment—where the British presence was still establishing itself—would have served as a reminder of the emotional toll that colonial life took on its settlers.

---

4. PERSONAL AND EMOTIONAL Impact:

The loss of Francis would have been particularly poignant for Sir Richard, as it occurred just after the Industrial Revolution had begun reshaping many aspects of life in Britain and her colonies. At a time when technological advancements were providing some measure of comfort and progress, personal losses such as this were still raw and unavoidable. Children's mortality rates were high, especially in colonies far from home, and the emotional strain of such an event would have been compounded by the difficulties of colonization and the challenges faced in raising a family in a new and often precarious environment.

CONCLUSION:

In 1826, Sir Richard Henry Bonnycastle would have felt the profound grief of losing his son, Francis, while navigating life in Upper Canada. This loss occurred in the context of an expanding British colonial presence in Canada, where the challenges of settlement, isolation, and limited medical care made such tragedies even more difficult to bear. The emotional weight of this loss would have deeply affected the Bonnycastle family, particularly as they coped with the distance from their homeland, England.

AT 35 YEARS OLD, IN 1827, Sir Richard Henry Bonnycastle experienced the joy of the birth of his daughter Henrietta on July 10, 1827, in Ontario, Canada. This event marked a new chapter in the Bonnycastle family's life, offering a sense of renewal and hope after the tragic loss of his son Francis in 1826.

Context in 1827:

1. Life in Ontario in 1827:

By 1827, Upper Canada (modern-day Ontario) was continuing its development as a growing British colony. The economy was still largely based on agriculture, but new settlements were beginning to emerge along with roads, canals, and other infrastructure projects. This was also a time of some political tension and societal change, with the Rebellions of 1837 in the near future, although these were still a decade away.

---

2. FAMILY LIFE AND Significance of Henrietta's Birth:

The birth of Henrietta would have been a significant event for Sir Richard and his wife Frances, especially after the difficult year in which they had lost their son Francis. Henrietta's arrival may have helped to heal some of the emotional wounds caused by that loss and provided a new sense of joy for the Bonnycastle family in their life in Upper Canada.

---

3. COLONIAL LIFE AND the Bonnycastle Family:

Given Sir Richard's military background and his role as a British officer in Upper Canada, it's likely that he and his family were part of the small but significant British expatriate community. Henrietta's birth occurred in a period when Upper Canada was still undergoing many changes, from infrastructure to the rise of a settler economy. The presence of military families in the colony, as well as officers like Sir Richard, meant that Henrietta was likely born into a society that straddled both colonial life and the rapidly changing global world.

---

4. CHALLENGES AND JOY in Colonization:

Sir Richard had already endured the loss of a child, so the arrival of Henrietta might have been a bittersweet event. It brought new life and hope, but it also continued the journey of raising a family far from their homeland in England. Life in Ontario during this time was not without its difficulties, including harsh winters, potential for illness, and the challenges of establishing a new life in a distant colony. However, the birth of a child was always a moment of personal happiness and a symbol of continuity in the face of these challenges.

---

5. HENRIETTA'S PLACE in the Family History:

The birth of Henrietta in 1827 represented the continuation of the Bonnycastle legacy in Canada. Given the historical context of Sir Richard's role in the Royal Engineers and his contributions to the early development of Ontario, Henrietta was part of a family deeply embedded in both military and colonial history. Her birth also marked another generation in the Bonnycastle lineage, ensuring the continuity of the family's presence in Canada for years to come.

CONCLUSION:

The birth of Henrietta in 1827 was a significant event for Sir Richard Henry Bonnycastle and his family, offering a moment of joy after the profound loss of his son Francis. It also marked the continuation of the Bonnycastle legacy in Upper Canada during a period of growth and change in the colony. Henrietta's arrival would have brought hope and renewal to a family that had endured the challenges of colonial life, offering a new sense of future and continuity in the face of adversity.

AT 37 YEARS OLD, SIR Richard Henry Bonnycastle welcomed the birth of his daughter Charlotte in England on May 21, 1829. This was a significant event in the Bonnycastle family's life, marking the continuation of their lineage, especially after having established their presence in Upper Canada.

Context in 1829:

1. Life in England in 1829:

In 1829, England was undergoing significant changes as the country navigated the industrial revolution. In 1829, George Stephenson's famous steam locomotive, The Rocket, made its successful journey, signaling a shift in transportation that would influence global trade and communications. England was also deeply entrenched in its empire-building activities, and the British Empire was still expanding its reach around the world, including Canada.

For Sir Richard, the birth of his daughter in England might have marked a return to his homeland for a brief period, as he had spent considerable time in Upper Canada by this point. This period could have been one of transition for him and his family, moving between the colonial world of Canada and the established British society in England.

---

2. FAMILY LIFE AND Significance of Charlotte's Birth:

The birth of Charlotte in England represented an important new chapter in the Bonnycastle family's story. By now, the family had already experienced the challenges of colonial life, including the loss of some children and the trials of a military life in a far-off land. The arrival of Charlotte in England could have been a symbolic return to their roots, and it may have brought a sense of continuity in the face of the many challenges they had encountered. The presence of a child in the family, especially after the loss of William and Francis, would have been a source of renewed hope and joy.

3. POLITICAL AND SOCIAL Climate in 1829:

In 1829, England was a nation in the midst of important reforms. The Catholic Emancipation Act was passed, allowing Catholics to hold public office, an important step in easing religious tensions in Britain. Meanwhile, the Industrial Revolution continued to reshape the country, with urbanization and technological advancements changing how people lived and worked. Sir Richard's military career would have placed him at the intersection of these societal shifts, with the demands of service in the Royal Engineers possibly pulling him between the old world of military tradition and the new, rapidly changing industrial landscape.

4. SIR RICHARD'S CONTINUED Role in the British Empire:

At this stage in his life, Sir Richard had already had significant military and colonial experiences. The birth of Charlotte could have symbolized a moment of personal reflection, especially with his service as a military officer in both Ireland and Canada. The family would have continued to balance their connections to Britain while managing life in the New World. The birth of another child in England would have reinforced their ties to their homeland, even as they established their place in Canada.

5. CHARLOTTE'S PLACE in the Bonnycastle Legacy:

As the daughter of a prominent British officer and the latest addition to the Bonnycastle family, Charlotte's birth in England reinforced the family's connection to both Britain and Canada. Her presence in the family lineage would help cement the Bonnycastle name as one that bridged both the colonial and imperial worlds. With Sir Richard's legacy in military service and his significant role in the development of Upper Canada, Charlotte would eventually play a part in continuing that legacy.

CONCLUSION:

The birth of Charlotte in 1829 marked a significant moment for Sir Richard Henry Bonnycastle and his family. It was a continuation of their legacy and a symbol of renewal after the losses they had suffered. With her birth in England, the family was able to reassert their ties to their homeland while navigating the challenges of colonial life in Canada. Charlotte's arrival not only brought joy but also added to the Bonnycastle family's enduring connection to both the British Empire and the growing Canadian colony.

AT 38 YEARS OLD, SIR Richard Henry Bonnycastle welcomed the birth of his daughter Catherine Anne Bonnycastle on December 18, 1829, in Kingston, Upper Canada (now Ontario). This was a significant moment for the Bonnycastle family, as it occurred in the very heart of the colony where Sir Richard had established himself and his career.

Context in 1829:

1. Life in Upper Canada (Kingston): By 1829, Upper Canada (modern-day Ontario) was an emerging colony in British North America, still under the strong influence of the British Crown. Kingston, strategically located at the confluence of the St. Lawrence River and Lake Ontario, was becoming a key military and

administrative hub. Sir Richard's involvement in military and engineering work in Kingston was pivotal, as the region was crucial for controlling access between the Great Lakes and the St. Lawrence Seaway.

Catherine Anne's birth would have been a significant event in Kingston, which, although small by modern standards, was a bustling and developing town with a growing population of settlers and military personnel. It was a time of both colonial stability and growing tension, particularly surrounding governance, land rights, and relations with the First Nations peoples in the region.

---

2. THE BONNYCASTLE Family in Upper Canada: Sir Richard had already experienced several years in Upper Canada by the time Catherine Anne was born. His military service with the Royal Engineers had solidified his status, and his family had become an important part of the social fabric in Kingston. Catherine's birth was one of joy, a new addition to a family already marked by significant milestones. Sir Richard had seen many changes in his life, from military postings to family tragedies, and this new life represented a fresh chapter in the family's ongoing story in Upper Canada.

---

3. POLITICAL AND SOCIAL Climate in 1829: In 1829, Upper Canada was still a province under British rule, with Lieutenant Governor Sir John Colborne overseeing its affairs. The colony was seeing slow but steady development, including the building of key infrastructure such as roads, fortifications, and settlements. The Royal Engineers, with whom Sir Richard served, were critical in shaping the landscape of both Upper Canada and the military presence in the region.

In terms of society, the colonial elite in Kingston, made up of military officers, government officials, and settlers, likely provided a stable environment for Catherine Anne to grow up. She would have been part of a family that played a key role in shaping the future of the province, with the Bonnycastle name already recognized for military expertise and colonial leadership.

---

4. PERSONAL IMPACT on Sir Richard: The birth of Catherine Anne marked a milestone in Sir Richard's personal life. At 38, Sir Richard was nearing the peak of his career in Upper Canada, yet he had already faced the complexities of being a father in a colonial setting. With several children born both in England and Canada, the addition of Catherine brought a sense of continuity to his family, especially after the losses of earlier children. His growing family symbolized both the enduring presence of the Bonnycastle legacy in the colony and the personal challenges of raising children in a far-off land.

---

5. LEGACY OF CATHERINE Anne: Catherine Anne Bonnycastle would become an integral part of the Bonnycastle family, which had a rich legacy of military and colonial contributions. Her birth in Kingston, a pivotal location for the military and political development of Upper Canada, connected her not only to her father's legacy but also to the expanding narrative of Canada as it slowly moved toward a more settled and governed society.

As the daughter of a prominent military figure, Catherine Anne would have been well-positioned to carry on the Bonnycastle name, whether through her involvement in the community or through family connections in later life.

CONCLUSION:

Catherine Anne Bonnycastle's birth on December 18, 1829, in Kingston, Upper Canada, symbolized both personal joy and the continuation of her family's legacy in the colony. As Sir Richard Henry Bonnycastle's daughter, she was born into a world of both military influence and colonial development. Her birth added to the family's rich history in Upper Canada, a place that would continue to shape both her future and the future of the province.

AT 41 YEARS OLD, SIR Richard Henry Bonnycastle welcomed the birth of his daughter Georgiana Bonnycastle in Kingston, Upper Canada, on July 19, 1832. Tragically, she passed away at just over one year old, on August 25, 1833, in York, Ontario (now Toronto).

Context in 1832-1833:

1. Life in Upper Canada (Kingston): By 1832, Kingston was a growing town that had become a key military and administrative center in Upper Canada. The town, located at the mouth of the Cataraqui River near Lake Ontario, was heavily influenced by the presence of military officers and British settlers, including figures like Sir Richard Henry Bonnycastle, who served with the Royal Engineers.

Kingston was evolving from a small military garrison to a developing urban center. The town, although relatively small, was vital in shaping the direction of the colony. Sir Richard would have been involved in various military and infrastructure projects, contributing to the region's growth and stability.

---

2. THE BONNYCASTLE Family and Georgiana's Birth: Georgiana Bonnycastle's birth in 1832 was another addition to the Bonnycastle family, which had already seen several children born in both England and Upper Canada. The birth of a child was an important event, especially for a family like the Bonnycastles, who were well-known in the colony's military and administrative circles.

Sir Richard, with his military background and role in Upper Canada, would have been deeply involved in his family's life, though the tragedy of Georgiana's early death would have brought deep sorrow to the family. The loss of a child was a common, albeit painful, experience in the 19th century, and such a loss would have been felt acutely by the Bonnycastle family, especially given their established social standing.

---

3. THE TRAGIC DEATH of Georgiana: Georgiana's death at just over a year old was an unfortunate reminder of the fragility of life during this era. Infant mortality was common in the 19th century due to the lack of modern medicine and the presence of diseases that could strike suddenly and without warning. The fact that she passed away in York (Toronto) suggests that the family may have been living or traveling in the area at the time.

The loss of a child during this time period, particularly at such a young age, was a tragic but not uncommon occurrence. Families were often forced to cope with such losses without the support of modern healthcare or understanding of the causes of disease. For Sir Richard, who had already experienced several child deaths, this loss would have been a painful chapter in his family's story.

---

4. IMPACT ON SIR RICHARD Henry Bonnycastle: At 41, Sir Richard was well-established in Upper Canada. However, the loss of

his daughter Georgiana would have been a personal sorrow amidst his professional and familial responsibilities. He had already faced the death of several children, and Georgiana's passing added to the series of family tragedies. It is possible that these losses affected his outlook on life, deepening his resolve in his military and engineering work as a means of leaving a lasting legacy for his surviving family members.

Sir Richard's role as a father was marked by both joy and loss. The Bonnycastle family's history was shaped by the deaths of several children, and the passing of Georgiana would have been a poignant reminder of the fragility of life in the colonial era.

---

5. LEGACY OF GEORGIANA: Although Georgiana did not live long, she was part of the Bonnycastle family's history in Upper Canada, and her memory would likely have been preserved by her family. For Sir Richard, the loss of a child like Georgiana may have deepened his resolve to secure his family's legacy, contributing to his continued efforts in his military and colonial work.

CONCLUSION:

The birth of Georgiana Bonnycastle in 1832 and her untimely death in 1833 marked a tragic chapter in the Bonnycastle family's story. The loss of an infant was a heart-wrenching experience for any family, particularly in the context of 19th-century Upper Canada, where life was often uncertain and fragile. For Sir Richard Henry Bonnycastle, this loss would have added to the personal challenges he faced as a father, but it also became part of the legacy of his family in a land that was still in the process of becoming a nation.

AT 42 YEARS OLD, SIR Richard Henry Bonnycastle welcomed the birth of his daughter Louisa Bonnycastle on November 11, 1833, in York, Ontario (now Toronto).

Context in 1833:

1. Life in York, Ontario (1833): By 1833, York was a small but growing town and a significant administrative center in Upper Canada. It was also the capital of the colony, a role it held until 1841 when it was replaced by Toronto. Despite its small size, York was a hub for trade and military activity and a focal point for British settlers, many of whom, like the Bonnycastle family, were tied to the colonial government and military.

Sir Richard and his family were likely well-established in the community, with Sir Richard's position as a military officer and engineer providing him both influence and standing. York was evolving, with the growth of infrastructure, homes, and roads, making it a bustling, though still developing, urban center.

---

2. THE BONNYCASTLE Family in York: Louisa Bonnycastle's birth marked the continuation of the Bonnycastle family in Upper Canada, following a string of other children, many of whom had passed away in infancy. Sir Richard, already a father of several children, including those who had tragically died in childhood, would have welcomed Louisa with hopes for a long and prosperous life.

For Lady Frances, Louisa's mother, it was also a moment of joy amidst the challenges of raising a large family in a frontier colony. The family would have continued to be involved in the colony's social and military life, with Sir Richard's role as a military engineer being key to his identity in the colony.

---

3. THE ROLE OF SIR Richard in 1833: By this point in his life, Sir Richard Henry Bonnycastle was a seasoned military officer, engineer, and a prominent figure in Upper Canada. His work included surveying and building infrastructure vital for the colony's defense and development. His military career, combined with his family life, placed him in the center of both the political and social spheres of Upper Canada.

---

4. THE SIGNIFICANCE of Louisa's Birth: Louisa's birth in 1833 was likely a moment of renewed hope for the Bonnycastle family. After the loss of several children, including Georgiana just a year prior, Louisa's arrival would have been welcomed with deep affection and prayers for her health and happiness. Sir Richard's life was marked by both professional success and personal tragedy, so the birth of a healthy child like Louisa would have been a blessing for the family, offering a glimmer of joy amidst earlier losses.

As a family of means and social standing, the Bonnycastles would have had access to better medical care and support, but infant mortality was still common during this period. Louisa's survival would have been a source of immense relief for Sir Richard and his wife, especially after their previous heartaches.

---

5. LEGACY AND IMPACT: Louisa Bonnycastle's birth would contribute to the growing legacy of the Bonnycastle family in Upper Canada, a legacy tied to both their military service and their involvement in the development of the region. Sir Richard, in particular, was dedicated to shaping the infrastructure and future of

the colony, and his family played a role in helping to cement the Bonnycastles' place in Upper Canada's history.

Louisa, as one of the last of Sir Richard's children born in Upper Canada, was likely a figure of great importance to her father. Sir Richard would have seen her not only as his child but also as part of the continuing effort to establish and secure his family's position in a rapidly changing world.

CONCLUSION:

The birth of Louisa Bonnycastle in 1833 came at a time of transition for the Bonnycastle family. It marked a moment of hope and renewal after the losses of previous children, including Georgiana. For Sir Richard, Louisa's arrival symbolized a new chapter, even as the world around him was shifting—York was evolving into Toronto, and Upper Canada was moving toward Confederation. Louisa would go on to become a part of the larger history of her family and the development of Ontario.

AT 45 YEARS OLD, SIR Richard Henry Bonnycastle would have been living through a time of significant upheaval and change in Upper Canada during the Upper and Lower Canadian Rebellions of 1837. These rebellions were a result of growing discontent among the colonists with the British colonial government and the entrenched elite, which led to uprisings in both Upper Canada (now Ontario) and Lower Canada (now Quebec).

Context of 1837 for Sir Richard:

1. Political and Social Climate: By 1837, tensions were rising in both Upper and Lower Canada due to dissatisfaction with the colonial

administration, particularly its unresponsiveness to demands for democratic reform. In Upper Canada, the Family Compact, a small group of elites, controlled the political and economic life of the colony. Many settlers, particularly the Reformers, felt excluded from power and frustrated by the lack of meaningful democratic representation.

---

2. THE UPPER CANADA Rebellion: The Upper Canada Rebellion was largely led by William Lyon Mackenzie, a journalist and politician who advocated for greater democratic rights for the people of the colony. The rebellion began in November 1837, when Mackenzie and his followers attempted to seize control of Toronto (then called York) in an effort to overthrow the government and establish a more representative government. The rebellion was swiftly suppressed by loyalist forces, and Mackenzie was forced to flee.

---

3. SIR RICHARD'S ROLE and Position: As a seasoned military officer and engineer, Sir Richard Henry Bonnycastle would have been in a position to witness, and possibly be involved in, the response to the rebellions. Given his established role in Upper Canada, it's likely that he would have supported the loyalist cause during the rebellions. His background in the military and his connections to the British authorities would have placed him at odds with the Reformers who sought more autonomy from the British government.

---

4. PERSONAL IMPACT: While Sir Richard was not one of the central figures in the rebellion, the uprisings would have affected his family life and his position in the colony. Upper Canada was a relatively small and close-knit society, and the political events of the time were impossible to ignore. It is possible that Sir Richard's military

background and his family's position within the colonial elite made him a figure of authority during the Rebellions, possibly aiding the government in quelling the insurgencies, either directly or indirectly.

The Bonnycastle family, being loyal to the British crown, would have been sympathetic to the colonial government's suppression of the rebellion. However, the rebellions may have also created an atmosphere of fear and uncertainty, especially given the political turmoil and the threat of more widespread unrest.

---

5. AFTERMATH OF THE Rebellions: After the rebellions, Upper Canada saw significant political changes, including the Act of Union in 1841, which merged Upper Canada and Lower Canada into a single colony, the Province of Canada. The Bonnycastle family's legacy and position within the colony would have been influenced by the post-rebellion restructuring, as the influence of the Family Compact waned, and new political dynamics emerged.

CONCLUSION:

At 45, Sir Richard Henry Bonnycastle found himself in the midst of one of the most tumultuous periods in Upper Canada's history. While not directly involved in the rebellions, his position as a military officer and his loyalty to the British Crown likely placed him on the side of the government during these uprisings. The Rebellions of 1837 had a profound impact on the colony, and the subsequent Act of Union would shape the future of Upper Canada and the Bonnycastle family's role within it. For Sir Richard, this period of unrest would have been a time of great personal and professional reflection as he navigated the changing political landscape.

AT 53 YEARS OLD, SIR Richard Henry Bonnycastle would have been deeply affected by the loss of his daughter Catherine Anne, who passed away on June 27, 1845, in York, Ontario (now Toronto). This would have been a significant personal tragedy, as the loss of a child, especially at such a young age, was a heart-wrenching experience for parents in the 19th century.

Context and Possible Impact on Sir Richard:

1. Emotional Impact: The death of Catherine Anne, at just 15 years old, would have been a devastating blow to the Bonnycastle family. As a father, Sir Richard would have experienced profound grief, compounded by the emotional toll of losing another child. It is noteworthy that, by this point, several of Sir Richard's children had passed away young, including his son Charles (who died as an infant) and his son Francis (who died at just 4 years old). Losing Catherine Anne, his surviving daughter from his later years, would have been especially painful.

---

2. SOCIAL AND FAMILY Effects: The loss of a child was not only a personal tragedy but also had broader social implications in a close-knit colonial community like York. The Bonnycastle family, being part of the colonial elite, would have faced this loss with a sense of public grief, though they might have also been supported by their social connections. Sir Richard's role in military, engineering, and colonial affairs would have required him to maintain a certain public demeanor, but his private sorrow over his daughter's death would have been significant.

---

3. PERSONAL REFLECTION: At 53, Sir Richard would have been reflecting on his life, both the successes and the challenges. He had already experienced a lengthy career, and his professional achievements, including his involvement with the military and the development of the colonial infrastructure, had made him a prominent figure in Upper Canada. Yet, with the death of his daughter, it's likely that he would have been confronted with the fragility of life and the weight of familial loss.

---

4. FAMILY LEGACY: THE Bonnycastle family had faced numerous challenges, including the deaths of several children, and Catherine Anne's death would have added to the weight of these losses. However, Sir Richard's legacy would likely have been focused on his contributions to the growth of Upper Canada, his military service, and his role in the development of key infrastructure projects. His surviving family members would have continued to carry his name and legacy, but the absence of Catherine Anne might have left a permanent mark on his personal life.

---

5. HEALTH AND REFLECTION on Mortality: By the time of his daughter's death, Sir Richard was in his early 50s, which in the 19th century was considered to be middle age. He might have been beginning to think more about his own mortality, particularly after losing several children and dealing with the social and political stresses of colonial life. This loss could have heightened his awareness of the fleeting nature of life and perhaps shifted his priorities in the years following.

CONCLUSION:

At 53, Sir Richard Henry Bonnycastle was confronted with the tragic loss of his daughter, Catherine Anne, a loss that would have impacted him deeply both emotionally and socially. This period in his life would have been marked by grief, reflection, and the challenge of navigating the personal toll of child loss while maintaining his role in the colonial establishment. The death of Catherine Anne added to the series of personal tragedies that would define Sir Richard's later years, shaping his legacy and the course of his family's history in Upper Canada.

AT 54 YEARS OLD, IN 1846, Sir Richard Henry Bonnycastle would have witnessed the patent of the sewing machine by Elias Howe. This invention marked a significant moment in industrial history, revolutionizing the textile industry by greatly increasing the speed and efficiency of garment production.

For Sir Richard, who was deeply involved in the colonial military and infrastructure development, this development would have been of interest as it signified the continued progress of technological innovations, which would have influenced both military and civilian industries. Though Sir Richard was not directly involved in the textile or manufacturing sectors, the sewing machine's potential to impact the workforce, especially in areas like clothing production and textile manufacturing, would have been significant for the economy of Upper Canada and beyond.

Broader Impact of the Invention:

1. Economic and Social Change: The sewing machine became a game-changer in the textile industry, reducing the time required for sewing garments and paving the way for mass production of clothing. In a colony like Upper Canada, where the economy was still largely

agricultural and based on small-scale industries, innovations like this would have played a role in shaping future industrial growth.

---

2. IMPACT ON SIR RICHARD'S World: Sir Richard might have viewed the invention of the sewing machine as part of the broader Industrial Revolution that was reshaping the world. As a military officer, engineer, and colonial administrator, he would have been aware of the shift towards mechanization in Europe and North America, even though his own immediate surroundings were still deeply rooted in agricultural and manual labor.

---

3. TECHNOLOGICAL ADVANCEMENTS: While the sewing machine's impact may not have been immediate in his daily life, Sir Richard would have been part of an era when the pace of technological innovation was accelerating. He had already seen advancements like the steam engine and the expansion of railroads, and the sewing machine was just another example of how technology was changing the fabric of society (both literally and figuratively).

IN CONCLUSION, AT 54, Sir Richard Henry Bonnycastle would have lived through an exciting period of technological change, where innovations like the sewing machine were beginning to change industries. As a colonial figure engaged in governance and military affairs, the practical effects of such inventions would have been felt in broader economic shifts, even though they were outside of his direct professional sphere.

SIR RICHARD HENRY BONNYCASTLE passed away on November 2, 1847, in Kingston, Canada West (now Ontario). His death occurred at the age of 56 and he was buried in St. Paul's Anglican Churchyard, Kingston, where many prominent figures of the time were laid to rest.

Context of His Passing:

By 1847, the region of Canada West (which later became Ontario) was undergoing significant changes. The Upper Canadian Rebellion of 1837 had already taken place, and the tensions of colonial life were beginning to shift towards the more stable period that would precede Confederation in 1867.

Sir Richard's passing marked the end of a life deeply involved in the shaping of Canada's early colonial military and infrastructure. His work in building military roads, his position as a military officer, and his role in the development of the fledgling colony would have left a lasting impact on the region.

Aftermath and Legacy:

St. Paul's Anglican Churchyard, where he is buried, remains a place of historical significance in Kingston. The church, established in the early 19th century, has been a significant religious and community center for the people of Kingston and beyond. His burial there links his legacy with the history of Kingston, which played a critical role as a military and administrative hub in the early years of Canada West.

His family, especially his daughters, would have continued to live through the changes of the 19th century, with Canada West undergoing profound shifts, including the push towards responsible government and eventual union with the other provinces to form Canada.

THOUGH SIR RICHARD Bonnycastle was no longer alive to see the full transformation of Canada, his contributions to its military and infrastructure remained significant, and his resting place in St. Paul's Anglican Churchyard continues to be a part of that legacy.

ELIZABETH BRAYLEY

ELIZABETH BRAYLEY[37]

Elizabeth Brayley was laid to rest on August 8, 1804, in Kingston, Upper Canada. Her grave became part of the grounds where St. Paul's Anglican Church was later constructed. This church remains a historic landmark, commemorating the early settlers who helped establish Kingston as a thriving colonial settlement.

Life in 1804:

Colonial Kingston: At the time of Elizabeth's death, Kingston was a small but significant Loyalist settlement. Established as a military and trading post, it was a hub for fur trade, shipbuilding, and agriculture. The population was modest, comprised mainly of Loyalist families who had fled the American Revolutionary War, Indigenous communities, and soldiers stationed at Fort Frontenac.

Community Development: Kingston was becoming more organized, with institutions such as churches, schools, and small businesses emerging to serve the growing community. The Anglican Church was central to social and spiritual life, providing not only religious services but also a gathering place for residents.

Daily Life: Residents lived in wooden or log homes, relying on subsistence farming, fishing, and small-scale trading. Life was labor-intensive, with women often managing households, producing textiles, and preserving food. Men typically worked as farmers, craftsmen, or laborers for the military or merchants.

Transportation and Trade: Kingston's location on Lake Ontario made it a vital transportation hub. Goods and people moved by water or over primitive roads, and the town's economy depended on trade with Montreal, other settlements in Upper Canada, and the United States.

Colonial Challenges: Life in Upper Canada was demanding, with settlers contending with harsh winters, limited medical care, and the constant threat of disease. Despite these challenges, the Loyalist spirit fostered resilience, and the community slowly expanded.

ELIZABETH'S BURIAL in 1804 reflects a time of hope and hard work, as Kingston transitioned from a frontier settlement into a more established colonial town. Her final resting place beneath St. Paul's Anglican Church connects her to the foundational history of one of Canada's oldest cities.

WILLIAM BRAYLEY

WILLIAM BRAYLEY[38]

William Brayley passed away in 1812 in Kingston, Ontario, and was buried in what is now the churchyard of St. Paul's Anglican Church, a site that later encompassed the graves of many early settlers.

Life in 1812:

War of 1812: This was a pivotal year, as war had just broken out between Britain and the United States. Kingston, a strategic military post on Lake Ontario, played a crucial role in the conflict. The town's residents would have been on high alert, with fortifications being built and soldiers stationed in the area.

Community Growth: Kingston was growing as a settlement, but it remained a small community with a mix of Loyalist families, soldiers, and traders. The economy revolved around agriculture, trade, and the military presence.

Daily Life: Residents lived modestly, with log or wooden frame homes. Daily life was centered on survival, with people farming, fishing, and bartering for goods. The Anglican Church played a vital role in the community, providing spiritual support during uncertain times.

Transportation: Travel and communication were slow, with goods and people transported by water or poorly maintained roads. Kingston's location made it a hub for lake-based transportation.

WILLIAM BRAYLEY'S BURIAL during this turbulent time reflects a community in transition, balancing the challenges of war and settlement expansion. His final resting place under St. Paul's Anglican Church symbolizes the foundational role of these early settlers in shaping Kingston's history.

GEORGE BRYANT U.E.L.

GEORGE BRYANT U.E.L.[39]

George Bryant, a United Empire Loyalist (UEL), was born around 1782 in Fort George, Niagara, Lincoln, Upper Canada, to Patrick Bryant and Sarah Ashmore. His birth situated him within the formative years of Upper Canada, a period marked by Loyalist resettlement and the early development of British-controlled territories following the American Revolutionary War.

Life in Upper Canada in the 1780s:

Loyalist Resettlement: George's parents, Patrick and Sarah, were among the Loyalists who fled the newly independent United States to seek refuge under British rule. These settlers were granted land and resources to establish new lives in Upper Canada, solidifying the region's British identity.

Fort George's Importance: Fort George, where George was born, was a pivotal military and civilian hub. It protected the Niagara River and served as a center for Loyalist settlements, trade, and defense.

Daily Life for Settlers: The Bryants, like other Loyalist families, faced the arduous task of clearing dense forests, building homes, and establishing farms. Farming was the primary livelihood, supplemented by hunting, fishing, and trading goods with Indigenous communities and other settlers.

Military Presence: The British military stationed at Fort George not only defended the area but also supported settlers by providing security and facilitating infrastructure development.

Indigenous Relations: Settlers often relied on the knowledge and assistance of local Indigenous peoples, who helped them navigate the unfamiliar landscape and survive. While trade and alliances were common, tensions arose as settlement expanded.

Community and Governance: Patrick and Sarah Bryant would have been part of the Loyalist efforts to create a structured community, bringing British customs, laws, and traditions to the area. The 1780s saw the establishment of the foundations for governance and order in Upper Canada.

AS THE SON OF PATRICK Bryant and Sarah Ashmore, George Bryant grew up in the early days of Upper Canada, experiencing both the hardships and opportunities that defined the Loyalist experience. His family's resilience and contributions helped shape the emerging identity of the province.

GEORGE BRYANT, UEL, was 9 years old in 1791 when the British Parliament passed the Constitutional Act, dividing the Province of Quebec into Lower Canada (modern-day Quebec) and Upper Canada (modern-day Ontario). This pivotal legislation marked the establishment of separate colonial governments to better address the distinct needs of French-speaking and English-speaking settlers.

Life in Upper Canada during 1791:

Formation of Upper Canada: The creation of Upper Canada provided a designated homeland for Loyalists like the Bryant family, reinforcing British customs, laws, and governance. It was a fresh start for families who had been uprooted during the American Revolutionary War.

Townships and Settlements: Loyalists, including George's family, contributed to the rapid growth of settlements, laying out townships and building communities. Fort George remained a critical hub for trade, military strategy, and civic activity.

Governance: The Constitutional Act introduced representative government. Each province had its own legislative assembly, providing settlers a voice in local affairs. In Upper Canada, this was the first step toward self-governance.

Everyday Challenges: The Bryants and other families faced the struggles of frontier life, including clearing land, farming, and managing relations with Indigenous communities, who were key allies but sometimes conflicted with settlers over land use.

Infrastructure and Growth: 1791 marked the beginning of efforts to build roads, bridges, and public buildings to support the growing population. The Niagara region was crucial to trade routes and military strategy.

THE DIVISION INTO LOWER and Upper Canada significantly impacted the Bryant family's life, as it ushered in a new phase of British colonial development. At the age of 9, George witnessed the transformation of his homeland into a structured and distinct colony, setting the stage for Upper Canada's unique identity within British North America.

GEORGE BRYANT, UEL, was 9 years old when his younger brother, James Bryant, was born on January 29, 1791, in Kingston, Upper Canada. The Bryant family, led by Patrick Bryant and Sarah Ashmore, was actively establishing their place in the burgeoning colony.

The birth of James coincided with a transformative period in colonial history. Kingston, then an important Loyalist settlement, was thriving as a hub of commerce and military activity. The family would have been deeply involved in the communal efforts to develop infrastructure, maintain farms, and build a strong foundation for future generations in Upper Canada.

As an older sibling, George likely took on responsibilities to assist his parents and help care for his younger siblings, including James, while adapting to life in the new colony amidst its challenges and opportunities.

GEORGE BRYANT, UEL, was 25 years old when slavery was abolished in the British colonies in 1807. This landmark legislation, known as the Abolition of the Slave Trade Act, marked a significant moral and societal shift across the British Empire.

In Upper Canada, the move toward abolition had already begun earlier with the Act to Limit Slavery passed in 1793, the first legislation in the British Empire to restrict the practice. By 1807, Upper Canada was transitioning away from reliance on enslaved labor, reflecting the growing global momentum against slavery.

As a resident of Kingston, a bustling Loyalist community, George would have witnessed these changes and the broader discussions about freedom and human rights. These events would have shaped the social and economic fabric of the colony, influencing the lives of settlers like the Bryant family as they adapted to the evolving world around them.

GEORGE BRYANT, UEL, was 39 years old when he passed away in 1821, leaving behind a legacy tied to the early Loyalist settlement of

Upper Canada. He was laid to rest in Kingston, Upper Canada, in what would later become the grounds of St. Paul's Anglican Church.

At the time of his death, Kingston was a thriving Loyalist town, serving as an important military and trade hub along the St. Lawrence River. The War of 1812 had ended just a few years earlier, and the region was undergoing a period of rebuilding and development. The construction of infrastructure and institutions, including churches like St. Paul's, reflected the settlers' efforts to establish permanent communities.

St. Paul's Anglican Church, built over George's grave, stands today as a reminder of Kingston's rich history and the contributions of Loyalist families like the Bryants to the region's development.

SOPHIA BRINDLE

SOPHIA BRINDLE[40]

Sophia Brindle passed away in 1813 in Kingston, Ontario. She was laid to rest in a location that would later become part of the grounds for St. Paul's Anglican Church, a prominent historical landmark in Kingston.

In 1813, Kingston was a growing settlement, still bearing the scars of the War of 1812, which had seen significant military activity in the region. The town was developing its role as a key administrative and military center for Upper Canada. The church's eventual construction over Sophia's grave links her to the legacy of the community's early growth, both through the church itself and through the Loyalist families who were integral to Kingston's establishment.

St. Paul's Anglican Church continues to stand as a symbol of Kingston's colonial past, and Sophia Brindle's burial site remains a part of that enduring history.

JOHN CAMP BROOKS

JOHN CAMP BROOKS[41]

John Camp Brooks passed away and was buried on November 7, 1809, in Kingston, Ontario. His final resting place is located where St. Paul's Anglican Church would later be constructed, a significant landmark in the city's history.

At the time of his death, Kingston was still a small but growing settlement in Upper Canada. The early 1800s were a formative period for the region, as it served as a crucial military post during the War of 1812, and the population was primarily made up of British Loyalists and military personnel. The area would eventually become an important administrative and trade hub.

The construction of St. Paul's Anglican Church in the early 19th century would have been a major event for the community, symbolizing the development of both Kingston's religious life and its role as an emerging urban center. The church, built over the graves of those like John Camp Brooks, connects the town's modern history to its early settlers and their influence on the city's growth.

RICHARD AND MARY BROWN

RICHARD AND MARY BROWN[42][43]

Richard and Mary Brown, a married couple, were buried in Kingston, Upper Canada, on November 26, 1795. Their graves are located where St. Paul's Anglican Church would eventually be built, placing them at the heart of a significant part of Kingston's history.

At the time of their death, Kingston was still developing as a British colonial settlement. The region was experiencing a steady influx of Loyalists and settlers after the American Revolution, and it was positioned as an important military and administrative center. In 1795, the town was still a relatively small community but growing in importance as a key point for trade and communication in Upper Canada.

The construction of St. Paul's Anglican Church in the early 19th century would later become a central landmark in Kingston. For Richard and Mary Brown, their burial site being built over by the church symbolizes the deep connection between Kingston's early settlers and the formation of the community's religious and civic life. The church, still standing today, continues to remind visitors of the region's early colonial roots and the individuals who contributed to its growth.

UNKNOWN BUCHETTE

UNKNOWN BUCHETTE[44][45]

Unknown Buchette and her child were buried on September 6, 1792, in Kingston, Upper Canada. Their graves are located beneath where St. Paul's Anglican Church would eventually be constructed, tying their final resting place to one of the city's most historic landmarks.

In 1792, Kingston was still a small settlement, largely inhabited by Loyalists and early European settlers. The town was beginning to take shape as a British colonial stronghold, with military and administrative importance growing as the years passed. The St. Lawrence River, which ran close to Kingston, made the town a strategic location for trade and defense.

The burial of Unknown Buchette and her child during this early period reflects the harsh realities of frontier life, where many families faced challenges from illness, difficult living conditions, and the threat of war or conflict. The fact that the mother and child were buried together suggests a shared fate, possibly due to disease or other hardships of the time.

Today, the site where their graves lay beneath St. Paul's Anglican Church remains a poignant reminder of the early struggles and lives lost in Kingston, marking their place in the broader story of the community's development in the late 18th century.

JOSEPH BURKE

JOSEPH BURKE[46]

Joseph Burke passed away in 1796 in Kingston, Upper Canada, and was laid to rest in the area where St. Paul's Anglican Church was later constructed. His grave, along with those of other early settlers, forms part of the foundation of this historic church, which has become a symbol of Kingston's early colonial roots.

During the time of Joseph Burke's death, Kingston was a growing community, still deeply influenced by the Loyalist settlers who had fled the American Revolution. In the 1790s, Kingston served as a strategic military and naval post, with British forces establishing their presence in the area. This period saw the expansion of infrastructure, with the construction of key buildings, including the early churches that would serve as centers of both faith and community life.

The establishment of St. Paul's Anglican Church, which was built over Burke's final resting place, marked the growth of Kingston as a town, and this church remains a significant landmark in the city's history. The Anglican faith was a cornerstone of British colonial life, and the church itself became a place not just for worship but also for marking milestones in the lives of early Kingston residents.

Joseph Burke's burial reflects the hardships and sacrifices of the early settlers, who often faced diseases, difficult living conditions, and the challenges of building a new life in a frontier settlement. His grave, like many others, is now part of Kingston's history, linking him to the broader story of this important colonial town.

ROBERT BURLEY

ROBERT BURLEY[47]

Robert Burley passed away in 1815 in Kingston, Upper Canada, and was buried in what would later become the grounds of St. Paul's Anglican Church. The church, constructed over the graves of early settlers like Robert, stands today as a testament to the lives of those who helped shape Kingston during its formative years.

In 1815, Kingston was a key military and naval town, emerging from the aftermath of the War of 1812, which had heightened its importance as a strategic location on the Great Lakes. The town's growth was tied to its status as a vital hub for British defense, as well as its role in the settlement of Loyalists following the American Revolution. This period was marked by the establishment of infrastructure and community institutions, including churches, which became central to both spiritual and social life.

St. Paul's Anglican Church, built over Burley's grave, was a focal point for the growing Kingston community, and its establishment reflected the increasing stability of the region. In a time when life was often difficult and uncertain, especially after the hardships of war, the church provided not only a place of worship but also a sense of continuity and order. As the years passed, it became an anchor for both the British settlers and the local Indigenous populations.

Robert Burley's burial is part of this larger narrative of Kingston's growth in the early 19th century, where the lives of individuals like him are interwoven with the broader development of Upper Canada. His resting place beneath St. Paul's Church is now a quiet reminder of the early residents whose contributions and sacrifices helped shape the history of the region.

SAMUEL BURLEY

SAMUEL BURLEY[48]

Samuel Burley was buried on August 26, 1802, in Kingston, Upper Canada, and his final resting place became part of the grounds where St. Paul's Anglican Church was later constructed. As with many others buried in the early cemetery, Samuel's grave lies beneath a building that symbolizes the growth and establishment of Kingston as an important town in the early 19th century.

In 1802, Kingston was still emerging as a key location in the early stages of Upper Canada's development. The town was an essential military post and served as a strategic site for both the British military and Loyalist settlers who had fled the United States following the American Revolution. This was a time when the area was transitioning from a frontier settlement to a more established colonial community.

St. Paul's Anglican Church, built in the early 19th century, was central to Kingston's development, and it played a vital role in the spiritual and social life of its inhabitants. The construction of the church itself reflected the town's growth and the establishment of a community in Upper Canada. The church, along with the cemetery, became a historical landmark that holds the stories of many who lived and contributed to the town's early history.

Samuel Burley's burial beneath this church links his memory with the broader narrative of Kingston's early settlers, whose lives and legacies helped shape the town's character in the years following the establishment of Upper Canada. His grave serves as a quiet tribute to the community's early residents and the foundational role they played in the development of Kingston and the surrounding region.

UNKNOWN BUSH

UNKNOWN BUSH[49]

Unknown Bush was buried on August 14, 1796, in Kingston, Upper Canada. Their grave, like many others, became part of the grounds that would later be occupied by St. Paul's Anglican Church. The burial reflects the early days of Kingston, which was a growing colonial town at the time.

In 1796, Kingston was still in its formative years following the influx of Loyalist settlers after the American Revolution. The town was becoming an important military and strategic location due to its proximity to the U.S. border and its role as a hub for both trade and military defense. As Upper Canada (modern-day Ontario) developed, communities like Kingston began to establish churches, schools, and other institutions to serve the growing population.

The establishment of St. Paul's Anglican Church in Kingston represented both religious and community growth in the region. As the church became a focal point for the community, the cemetery where Unknown Bush was buried became a place of reverence and remembrance for the early settlers and their descendants. Although the identity of Unknown Bush remains a mystery, their resting place remains part of the historical fabric of Kingston, which was slowly transforming into a significant colonial town at the time.

JOHN BUTTERWORTH

JOHN BUTTERWORTH[50]

John Butterworth was born in 1792, likely in one of the early settlements of Upper Canada, which was a part of British North America at the time. This period in history was marked by significant changes and challenges for settlers in Canada.

In 1792, the political landscape was shaped by the recent creation of the provinces of Upper and Lower Canada in 1791, following the division of the Quebec Province. These changes were part of efforts to better govern the growing number of Loyalist settlers, who had fled the American Revolution. As Upper Canada (now Ontario) was being populated, towns like Kingston and York (now Toronto) were emerging as key centers for settlement, trade, and governance.

The early 1790s also saw the establishment of key institutions such as churches, schools, and other public services that would support the growth of the colony. For settlers like John Butterworth, life during this period involved a pioneering spirit, with many engaging in agriculture, trade, and military service, and some were connected to the burgeoning infrastructure of the province.

While little specific information is available about John Butterworth at this time, his birth in 1792 places him at the heart of Upper Canada's early years. The decade following his birth would have been one of both hardship and opportunity as the Loyalist legacy began to take root in the region.

JOHN BUTTERWORTH AND Abigail Reid's daughter, Isabella Butterworth, was born in Kingston, Ontario on May 18, 1819. Kingston, at the time, was a rapidly growing town that played a key role in the early history of Ontario and Upper Canada.

In 1819, Kingston was transitioning from a military and administrative center to a more developed community. The town was situated on the shores of Lake Ontario and served as an important location for trade and military operations due to its strategic position. Kingston had become the capital of Upper Canada from 1815 to 1841, until it was moved to York (later Toronto).

As for the Butterworth family, life during this time would have been shaped by the growing sense of British colonial identity, and Kingston was a place where both military personnel and settlers coexisted. The community was diverse, including settlers who had arrived as part of the Loyalist migration and those who came in search of new opportunities.

Isabella, born in 1819, would have experienced a Kingston that was in the midst of shaping its future, with developing infrastructure, institutions like St. George's Church (founded in 1819), and a burgeoning sense of community. The early 19th century was a time of both growth and uncertainty for many in Upper Canada, and the Butterworths, like other families, were likely part of the foundational group of settlers who helped shape the area during its early years.

AT 29 YEARS OLD, IN 1821, John Butterworth would have witnessed a major shift in the fur trade industry with the merger of the Hudson's Bay Company (HBC) and the North West Company (NWC). This merger consolidated the two dominant fur trading companies in Canada, creating a monopoly on the fur trade that greatly affected the economy and society of the time. While this event primarily impacted those directly involved in the fur trade, it was a significant moment in the history of British North America.

During this period, Kingston was a hub for commerce and trade, located at the confluence of Lake Ontario and the St. Lawrence River, which made it a strategic port for settlers, traders, and military personnel. While John Butterworth worked as a hatter, which suggests he was involved in the making and selling of hats—likely a craft that catered to the needs of the growing population of settlers, soldiers, and civilians—he would have been affected indirectly by the economic changes brought about by the merger. The economic shift could have impacted the availability of resources and the demand for goods, which would, in turn, influence businesses like John's.

The merging of these two fur trading giants, along with other political and economic developments in early 19th-century Canada, shaped the region's growth. Kingston, being a key military and economic center during this time, also saw increased infrastructure development, which would have provided opportunities for local businesses like hat-making to flourish. Given his profession, John likely benefited from the growing town's prosperity, as demand for everyday goods and services increased.

AT 30 YEARS OLD, JOHN Butterworth would have been navigating a period of significant change in both his personal life and the broader historical context. His daughter, Anne, was born on August 31, 1822, in Kingston, Ontario, during a time when the town was evolving both socially and economically.

Kingston was rapidly growing as a center of trade, military activity, and settlement. The population was expanding, and with the construction of important infrastructure like the Rideau Canal (which was completed in 1832), Kingston was becoming increasingly connected to other parts of Upper Canada. The economic climate was shifting as well, with the British North American colonies becoming more self-sufficient and developing a more diverse economy, partly influenced by the recent merger of the Hudson's Bay Company and the North West Company in 1821.

For John, a hatter by trade, this would have been a time of both opportunity and competition. As the town grew, so did the demand for goods and services, including clothing and accessories such as hats. With the increased prosperity in Kingston, it's likely that his business would have seen some growth. At the same time, he might have faced new challenges as a father, with his young family growing in a rapidly changing world. His daughter, Anne, would have been part of the next generation that would see Kingston's transformation into a major urban center in Ontario.

This year also marked a period of transition in the larger context of Upper Canada, as many settlers were finding their place in a society that was shifting from colonial rule toward greater self-governance. As a father and business owner, John Butterworth would have been focused on providing for his family, while also observing the changes around him as the social and economic fabric of the region continued to evolve.

AT THE AGE OF 42, JOHN Butterworth passed away on August 21, 1834, in Kingston, Ontario. His death occurred during a period of significant growth and change for both the town and the larger Canadian context. Kingston was becoming a vital hub of commerce and military importance. The early 1830s saw increased development, including the completion of the Rideau Canal, which connected

Kingston to Ottawa and beyond, fostering trade and economic expansion.

John's death, which happened just a few years after the 1821 merger of the Hudson's Bay Company and the North West Company, occurred in a period of change for the fur trade and economy in Upper Canada. Though John was a hatter, the broader regional economy was shifting toward more diversified industries as the influence of the fur trade began to wane.

He was buried in St. Paul's Anglican Churchyard, which would later be the site of St. Paul's Anglican Church—an enduring monument to the early settlers of Kingston. His final resting place in this churchyard links him to a pivotal moment in Kingston's history, as the town was growing in prominence and shaping its place in the expanding province of Canada. As a father of multiple children, including his daughter Isabella, who was born in 1819, and Anne, born in 1822, John's life and legacy would have contributed to the early development of the town and the emerging fabric of the Canadian settler community.

By the time of his passing, Kingston was well on its way to becoming a bustling, dynamic town, and the influence of people like John Butterworth—who worked as a skilled tradesman and supported his family during these transformative years—would have helped shape the character of the community.

---

[1] https://www.wikitree.com/wiki/Boileau-343#Ancestors

[2] https://www.wikitree.com/wiki/Atkinson-7786#Ancestors

[3] https://www.wikitree.com/wiki/Atkinson-7786#Ancestors

[4] https://www.wikitree.com/wiki/Atkinson-7787#Ancestors

[5] https://www.wikitree.com/wiki/Atkison-44#Ancestors

[6] https://www.wikitree.com/wiki/Austin-9694#Ancestors

[7] https://www.wikitree.com/wiki/Austin-9695#Ancestors

[8] https://www.wikitree.com/wiki/Aykroud-1#Ancestors

[9] https://www.wikitree.com/wiki/Badgley-241#Ancestors

[10] https://www.wikitree.com/wiki/Badgley-242#Ancestors

[11] https://www.wikitree.com/wiki/Bain-2447#Ancestors

[12] https://www.wikitree.com/wiki/Baker-37449#Ancestors

[13] https://www.wikitree.com/wiki/Baker-37450#Ancestors

[14] https://www.wikitree.com/wiki/Baker-37451[1]

[15] https://www.wikitree.com/wiki/Balfour-1322#Ancestors

[16] https://www.wikitree.com/wiki/Ballan-22[2]

[17] Charles Bamford (-abt.1826) | WikiTree FREE Family Tree[3]

[18] John Barnes (-bef.1803) | WikiTree FREE Family Tree[4]

[19] Jane Barns (-bef.1803) | WikiTree FREE Family Tree[5]

[20] https://www.wikitree.com/wiki/Barrice-1[6]

[21] John Bateman (-abt.1811) | WikiTree FREE Family Tree[7]

1. https://www.wikitree.com/wiki/Baker-37451#Ancestors

2. https://www.wikitree.com/wiki/Ballan-22#Ancestors

3. https://www.wikitree.com/wiki/Bamford-398#Ancestors

4. https://www.wikitree.com/wiki/Barnes-16409#Ancestors

5. https://www.wikitree.com/wiki/Barns-568#Ancestors

6. https://www.wikitree.com/wiki/Barrice-1#Ancestors

7. https://www.wikitree.com/wiki/Bateman-2686#Ancestors

[22] https://www.wikitree.com/wiki/Baymans-1[8]

[23] https://www.wikitree.com/wiki/Bayman-17[9]

[24] Adam Beard (-bef.1805) | WikiTree FREE Family Tree[10]

[25] Antoine Martin Beaubien (1765-bef.1800) | WikiTree FREE Family Tree[11]

[26] https://www.wikitree.com/wiki/Beeman-752[12]

[27] https://www.wikitree.com/wiki/Belfleur-1[13]

[28] https://www.wikitree.com/wiki/Betson-37[14]

[29] https://www.wikitree.com/wiki/Betton-58[15]

[30] https://www.wikitree.com/wiki/Blackwood-755[16]

[31] https://www.wikitree.com/wiki/Blain-616[17]

[32] https://www.wikitree.com/wiki/Bloom-1738[18]

[33] https://www.wikitree.com/wiki/Bointon-13#Ancestors

[34] https://www.wikitree.com/wiki/Bointon-12[19]

[35] https://www.wikitree.com/wiki/Bonnycastle-4[20]

---

8. https://www.wikitree.com/wiki/Baymans-1#Ancestors
9. https://www.wikitree.com/wiki/Bayman-17#Ancestors
10. https://www.wikitree.com/wiki/Beard-4452#Ancestors
11. https://www.wikitree.com/wiki/Beaubien-327#Ancestors
12. https://www.wikitree.com/wiki/Beeman-752#Ancestors
13. https://www.wikitree.com/wiki/Belfleur-1#Ancestors
14. https://www.wikitree.com/wiki/Betson-37#Ancestors
15. https://www.wikitree.com/wiki/Betton-58#Ancestors
16. https://www.wikitree.com/wiki/Blackwood-755#Ancestors
17. https://www.wikitree.com/wiki/Blain-616#Ancestors
18. https://www.wikitree.com/wiki/Bloom-1738#Ancestors
19. https://www.wikitree.com/wiki/Bointon-12#Ancestors
20. https://www.wikitree.com/wiki/Bonnycastle-4#Ancestors

[36] https://www.wikitree.com/wiki/Bonnycastle-3#Ancestors

[37] https://www.wikitree.com/wiki/Brayley-207[21]

[38] William Brayley (-abt.1812) | WikiTree FREE Family Tree[22]

[39] https://www.wikitree.com/wiki/Bryant-20194

[40] https://www.wikitree.com/wiki/Brindle-319[23]

[41] https://www.wikitree.com/wiki/Brooks-15071#Ancestors

[42] https://www.wikitree.com/wiki/Brown-85233#Ancestors

[43] https://www.wikitree.com/wiki/Unknown-605959#Ancestors

[44] https://www.wikitree.com/wiki/Buchette-2#Ancestors

[45] https://www.wikitree.com/wiki/Buchette-1[24]

[46] https://www.wikitree.com/wiki/Burke-7210#Ancestors

[47] https://www.wikitree.com/wiki/Burley-909#Ancestors

[48] https://www.wikitree.com/wiki/Burley-910#Ancestors

[49] https://www.wikitree.com/wiki/Burley-910#Ancestors

[50] https://www.wikitree.com/wiki/Butterworth-786#Ancestors

21. https://www.wikitree.com/wiki/Brayley-207#Ancestors

22. https://www.wikitree.com/wiki/Brayley-173#Ancestors

23. https://www.wikitree.com/wiki/Brindle-319#Ancestors

24. https://www.wikitree.com/wiki/Buchette-1#Anceestors

Don't miss out!

Visit the website below and you can sign up to receive emails whenever Angeline Gallant publishes a new book. There's no charge and no obligation.

https://books2read.com/r/B-A-QGSI-JZLIF

Also by Angeline Gallant

A Dragon's Diary
Dreaming of Dragons

Blood and Spirit Saga
The Rising Wind

Calling Her Heart
Whisper of the Heart
Calling Her Heart Volumes 1 & 2: A Small Town Romance Collection
No Turning Back
Calling Her Heart volumes 3 & 4
Forsake Me Not
Hear My Cry

FORGET ME NOT
Victoria, Ontario's Babies 1894 - 1895

Guardian of the Heart
Fallen Petals

Keeper Of Secrets
A Lady's Secret

Kingston's Love Chronicles
Springtime Promises

Midnight's Awakening
Heart of the Storm
Walking Through The Storm
Walking Through The Storm
Fighting the Storm
Call Me Cursed
Heart of the Storm

Secrets of the Underworld
Deklan's Dragons

Tell My Story Collection
Tell My Story: Germany 1851
Tell My Story: England 1852

Whispers From The Garrison Church

The Dervock Legacy
Echoes of Dervock

The Grave Whisperer
German Prisoners of War in Canada
Cataraqui United Church Cemetery
Whispers of Kingston
Wedding Bells in Kingston, Ontario, Canada 1923
St. Paul's Anglican Churchyard A-B
St. Paul's Anglican Churchyard C-D
St. Paul's Anglican Churchyard E - F
St. Paul's Anglican Churchyard G - H
St. Paul's Anglican Churchyard J - N
St. Paul's Anglican Churchyard O - R
St. Paul's Anglican Churchyard S - T
St. Paul's Anglican Churchyard, Kingston, Ontario T - Z
Small Graveyards & Burial Grounds: Kingston, Ontario, Canada
Cataraqui United Church Cemetery 1
Cataraqui United Church Cemetery 2
Cataraqui United Church Cemetary 3
Cataraqui United Church Cemetery 4
Cataraqui United Church Cemetery 5
Beth Israel Cemetery
Cataraqui United Church Cemetery 6
Beneath the Surface: Echoes from Beth Israel Cemetery
Grave Tales: Discovering the Lives of Beth Israel
Whispers Beneath St. Paul's
Unveiled

The Timeless Veil
Eternal Devotion

The Wolf Whisperer Series
Captured Heart
Fate's Legacy
Mohawk Valley
Cry of a Warrior
Wolf Whisperer volumes 1 & 2
Endless White
The Wolf Whisperer volumes 1 & 2

Timeless
The Time Keeper's Sanctuary

Timeless Whispers of Dervock Saga
Secrets of Dervock

Standalone
Winds of Change vol 1-3

Watch for more at https://www.goodreads.com/author/show/19703964.Angeline_Gallant.

About the Author

Angeline Gallant traces her roots through generations of Old Stock Canadian heritage, her passion for genealogy as deep and enduring as the forests and fields her ancestors once walked. With a reverence for history and an eye for detail, she weaves stories from the fragments of lives left behind in letters, records, and weathered headstones.

An avid reader and devoted writer, Angeline brings the past to life with a curiosity for heraldry and a deep love for the landscapes that shaped her family's story. Each name and date she uncovers feels less like history and more like coming home, a familiar echo in the vast tapestry of time. For her, these stories are not forgotten—they live, breathing in the quiet spaces of memory and tradition, a testament to lives once lived, now eternal in the pages of her books.

Read more at https://www.goodreads.com/author/show/19703964.Angeline_Gallant.

About the Publisher

At Crest & Quill Press, we bring history to life, one story at a time. Specializing in genealogy, heraldry, and historical fiction and nonfiction, we are passionate about uncovering the past and celebrating the stories that shape our world today.

From tales of noble lineages and family legacies to immersive historical sagas, our books are crafted for readers who crave a deeper connection to their roots and a richer understanding of history. Whether you're exploring the crests of your ancestors or diving into vivid narratives of bygone eras, Crest & Quill delivers stories that resonate and endure.

With a dedication to authenticity, storytelling, and the preservation of history, Crest & Quill Press is your gateway to the past—and a celebration of its impact on the present and future.

www.ingramcontent.com/pod-product-compliance
Lightning Source LLC
LaVergne TN
LVHW050546160826
845677LV00011B/2192

* 9 7 9 8 2 3 0 2 4 1 3 4 8 *